# Understanding Facial Recognition Difficulties in Children

*also in this series*

**Understanding Dyspraxia**
A Guide for Parents and Teachers (2nd Edition)
*Maureen Boon*
ISBN 978 1 84905 069 2

**Understanding Motor Skills in Children with Dyspraxia, ADHD, Autism, and Other Learning Disabilities**
A Guide to Improving Coordination
*Lisa A. Kurtz*
ISBN 978 1 84310 865 8

**Understanding Nonverbal Learning Disabilities**
A Common-Sense Guide for Parents and Professionals
*Maggie Mamen*
ISBN: 978-1-84310-593-0

**Understanding Regulation Disorders of Sensory Processing in Children**
Management Strategies for Parents and Professionals
*Pratibha Reebye and Aileen Stalker*
ISBN 978 1 84310 521 3

# Understanding Facial Recognition Difficulties in Children

Prosopagnosia Management Strategies
for Parents and Professionals

*Nancy L. Mindick*

*Foreword by Glenn Alperin*

Jessica Kingsley *Publishers*
London and Philadelphia

First published in 2011
by Jessica Kingsley Publishers
116 Pentonville Road
London N1 9JB, UK
and
400 Market Street, Suite 400
Philadelphia, PA 19106, USA
*www.jkp.com*

**Library of Congress Cataloging in Publication Data**
A CIP catalog record for this book is available from the Library of Congress

**British Library Cataloguing in Publication Data**
A CIP catalogue record for this book is available from the British Library

ISBN 978 1 84905 802 5

Printed and bound in Great Britain

MIX
Paper from responsible sources
FSC
www.fsc.org    FSC® C013604

# CONTENTS

# ACKNOWLEDGEMENTS

Special thanks go to "Donna Peterson," Jim Cooke, and Glenn Alperin, for their extensive interviewing and input related to the book. I truly hope that I have done justice to your interviews and feedback. Also to Jenni Welch and "Lydia Mathers" for thoughtful responses.

In addition, thanks to Liz Kolodney for encouraging true voice and Martha Hall for encouraging true compass, to Ellie Drago-Severson for encouragement to move forward, Jan Seymour Ford of Perkins School for the Blind for offering information related to vision. Thanks also to Howard Gardner for ideas about publishing, to Amy Rosoff Sampson for thoughtful comments at the project's beginning and Abigail Marshall for sharing with me the gift of compassion... and for reading. Thanks to Jennifer Dobbins for encouraging courage. To Ann Dowker, Anne Ipsen, and Maria Balestrieri, Rebekah Cotton, and Sharon Ware for thoughtful feedback. With warm gratitude to my editor, Helen Ibbotson, for insight, kindness, patience. To all people who kindly filled out interview questions and also who submitted photos, even if they were not used. Thanks also to Rachel Menzies and Claire Cooper for their insight and contributions.

I wish to also acknowledge every instructor or professor that I have ever had at Salus University. I have loved your effective, well-organized classes related to vision. Dr. M., thank you for nurturing a curiosity and for instilling knowledge, for living the motto (and therefore modeling) that true science is about the pursuit of an idea and the beauty of complexity. Thanks also to Barbara Jennings for general support and encouragement. Thank you to Mike May and other interviewees regarding the evolution of senses paper, because that work has in some ways informed this. Krista Anderson for encouragement, spirit. To Cousin Holly B. Ranieri for encouragement and resilience. To Rebecca Williams Jackson for professional expertize regarding the chapter on diagnosis and testing. Thanks also to the professors and researchers who kindly clarified regarding their research. To my dear friends, Wolfgang Laskowski and his wife, Dorothea, for kindness and wisdom, intelligence. Thank you to Dr. R.G. for your important, challenging feedback.

Although many were extremely helpful at various points in the writing process, the opinions expressed in this book represent only my own.

# FOREWORD

Not very long ago, there were only 200 documented cases of prosopagnosia in the whole world. Times have definitely changed. The last 14 years have produced enormous growth in understanding and awareness of prosopagnosia. When I first launched my personal website about prosopagnosia in October 1996, researchers understood that the condition was caused by either a brain injury, a stroke, or a severe infection. My hopes at that time were essentially twofold: I wanted to tell people what it was like to experience prosopagnosia from an insider's perspective, and I also wanted to reach out and possibly befriend others who also had prosopagnosia, thereby creating the opportunity to share ideas, thoughts, and experiences with people in similar circumstances who would understand, based on their own personal experience.

Current research, which Nancy has cited so eloquently in this book, suggests that the prevalence of prosopagnosia may be as high as 2 percent of the population as a whole. Perhaps more puzzling is that people with prosopagnosia seem to experience it differently—some of us being more severely affected by our own manifestations of the condition than others.

With that in mind, this book presents a significant overview of some thoughts and questions to consider in an effort to help children navigate the wide range of complex social situations they may encounter, both in a schooling environment and in the real world. It also contains a large number of tips as to how you might guide the prosopagnosic child and those they encounter toward safer, smoother, and less stressful social interactions.

You will get the most use out of this book if you use it more as a guide than an encyclopedia. After reviewing the circumstances of your situation, only you will know what is the best approach to take. You need to be open-minded and willing to explore what works and what doesn't for your child. You will find that this book provides a solid foundation from which to begin your exploratory journey with a child who may need help ranging from miniscule to significant. Either way, thank you so much for caring for the social and emotional well-being of the child in your life.

*Glenn Alperin, March, 2010*

# INTRODUCTION

What do I see when I see a face? And what do you see when you see a face? I can take you to the moon and back, but how will we tell each other what we saw there? If I tell you my experience, will you understand it, truly?

The expression, "He's just another face in the crowd" is a figure of speech, but for the prosopagnosic child it can be literally true. The individual with the severe face recognition deficit known as prosopagnosia may interact with another for six hours on a Monday and by Tuesday evening be unable to recognize that person on the street. This cognitive visual deficit is not about "acuity" (which could be resolved with glasses). Rather, it is related to how the brain processes faces, just as dyslexia influences reading, even if the individual is normal or even talented in many other areas.

I recall the day that I spent at an orientation picnic at Harvard Graduate School of Education. Most who were there sitting on the grass had appeared to me to be strangers, although I had already met some of them during gatherings at the school. As a woman with prosopagnosia and an educator for years, I had been quite accustomed to navigating crowds, organizing school activities, and having fun in an academic environment, but I have to admit that I found the orientation days to be somewhat—*well*—disorienting.

As an English as a Second Language teacher, I had been accustomed to having confidence in my ability to identify others by creating opportunities to ask such questions as "What is your name?," make seating charts, and lead activities. However, this was different: in a new university environment, anyone could show up in the library at any time, and each person could potentially be a student I had already met, a complete stranger, a teaching fellow, a staff member, or a professor for one of my classes. Smiling at those I didn't think I knew was helpful, but it left me feeling extremely lonely. I wondered whether I was ever going to genuinely "know" my classmates in the amorphous environment of graduate school.

But now I had left my assigned orientation group and was in line for a sandwich when someone ahead of me turned. As one of a percentage of prosopagnosics who can recognize when I'm being recognized, because I perceive facial expressions well, I realized that this woman "knew me," was giving me what I call a "hello look." Could she be someone whom I had met in passing or had spoken with during an information session? Had I never talked with her or was she perhaps a staff member? Then she spoke: "Hi, Nancy, I'm Alison. We had dinner together last night."

I was shocked. Alison? This was Alison, with whom I had spoken for hours the evening before. We had sat in close proximity in an outdoor café as daylight gave way to twilight, and I hadn't known now who she was.

I had decided to "come out" about the prosopagnosia when I returned for my Master's, because I reasoned that those with whom I would be interacting were educators and could understand the face recognition deficit. Nonetheless, realizing that I could have simply smiled at someone with whom I had extensively talked left me wondering as to how many others I had passed without acknowledging.

I have to admit that I may actually be a little unusual in that most of the time I don't mind being prosopagnosic. I'm thankful for my "cognitive home," and I think that the memories and perceptive experiences that we have are integral, important to who we are, worthy of honoring. I believe that culture is not only about the world around us, the norms with which we grow in societies, but also about the world within us, the cognitive comfort of our known perceived and imagined worlds, to the extent that they are limited and made possible by our biology.

As was the case with dyslexia, developmental prosopagnosia went largely unacknowledged for many years, despite its apparent widespread prevalence. Face recognition deficit was considered to be an extremely rare and seldom documented phenomenon that could result from brain injuries such as blows to the head or car accident trauma. Some people with a history of stroke were said to have acquired it.

Such was the case when I was tested for prosopagnosia in 2001. Following the advent of the internet, an increasing number of people had begun to communicate about severe face recognition problems, and it eventually became apparent to some with this deficit, along with researchers, that prosopagnosia could also occur from childhood, as a phenomenon "developmental" in nature. By 2002 the possible genetic basis for developmental prosopagnosia was a topic at a poster session offered at the European Congress of Human

Genetics in Strasbourg (Kennerknecht *et al.* 2002). Then, in 2006, a study published in American Journal of Genetics Part A (Kennerknecht *et al.* 2006) that this phenomenon impacts approximately two 2 percent of the population. Although the findings will need to be many times replicated , they do appear to be corroborated by other laboratories. In any case, if more than one family member has prosopagnosia, this may help to explain as to why there is a potential for parents to miss identifying the deficit, given its normalcy in some families.

Not all children who have prosopagnosia suffer as a result of it, and, in fact, some thrive socially. I myself love the dynamic of social interactions and have intentionally sought work that involves being with people. And there are prosopagnosics who find that face recognition deficit has a minimal impact only on their lives. However, this book is written to address the needs of those who become socially isolated as a result of the deficit. My hope is to offer some ideas for those who care about the prosopagnosic child and wish to have some insight into how to offer identity and social cues to those who need them. A child who realizes that his face perception skills are limited might be able to find alternative strategies for helping those in his life to feel "recognized," "known." One who lacks the ability to perceive emotional expressions may be able to elicit relevant information using non-facial strategies. And his helpers may learn to offer relevant information. To put it simply, if the pedagogy catches up with the research, if those adults who influence children's lives have greater understanding as to what the deficit is, then those parents and professionals wishing to include the prosopagnosic child will be more effective in doing so.

Personally, I believe that face recognition deficit is simply another manifestation of the cognitive diversity that characterizes us as a species, and the opportunity to address it a chance to act on our understanding of the talent differences crucial to functioning communities. I also believe that face perception is not only integrally linked to social talent, but to other areas of our understanding, as described in Chapter 4 and in the Appendix, which offers a simplified version of a theory that I developed in 2002 and continued to expand upon during some of my Master's coursework.

Regarding pronoun references in this book, I have chosen to use the male "he" for this Introduction, the female "she" for Chapter 1, etc. This is for several reasons. First, there are studies to suggest that the research into autistic spectrum disorders, which are sometimes associated with prosopagnosia, is male dominated, in terms of who is getting diagnosed, as researchers such as those at an International Association for Autism Research Conference (2009) have noted. With less knowledge of how being on the spectrum impacts girls, according to some research, there has been a later diagnosis and treatment for girls, as Van Baker has noted (2010). I do not wish to perpetuate the genderization of that research. I think that we all need to keep our eyes open to the fact that while it is possible for  prosopagnosia to manifest differently in males and females, it does impact individuals of both sexes.  In addition, I believe that if the goal of a book is to advocate for inclusion, it is crucial to use language that is, inherently, inclusive.

I have sometimes changed the names of individuals in the book, at their request, and I have also changed the names of people in their stories. But the people and their stories are real. In quoting interviewees, I will offer first and last names in the initial quote and only the first name in subsequent quotes from that person.

It is with hopes that the experiences I have had as a prosopagnosic on both sides of the classroom podium—as teacher and as student—as an individual who comprehends emotional expressions but who does not comprehend faces, will enable me to help narrow the distance between scientific research and pedagogy.

Chapter 1

# THE WORLD OF PROSOPAGNOSIA

## DEVELOPMENTAL PROSOPAGNOSIA

> Now anybody that I knew inside the school, I could not recognize
> outside the school. If any of these people were outside, I couldn't
> recognize them. I only recognized them, like Judy Maguire, who came
> out of her house, in other words…if she came out of her house every
> day, then I knew who it was… I knew her name was Judy Maguire.
> But if I saw her anyplace else, I wouldn't know who it was… (Donna
> Peterson, developmental prosopagnosic)

In order to begin to comprehend the challenges of developmental prosopagnosia, it is useful to explore how face recognition deficit from childhood
differs from that acquired after an individual has previously lived with face
recognition skills.

The child with developmental prosopagnosia is typically unaware that
her face recognition ability is significantly different from that of her peers.
Although Donna, quoted above, used context of place to glean information
about her friend's identity, it is unlikely that she was conscious of the strategy that she was using. Indeed, had an adult asked her whether she could
recognize faces, she probably would have responded affirmatively because
she could easily point to her own eyes, nose, and mouth, as well as those of
others. In fact, however, had Judy, emerged from a different house, Donna
may not have been able to recognize her friend, as she revealed during the
interview. Such non-facial clues as context of time or place, hair color, and/
or gait, as well as others to be discussed in Chapter 6, become a child's main

clues for gleaning identity, even though these sources of information are more transient and time-consuming to employ than are the more typical facial clues for those who are born with the ability to recognize them.

A kind of "invisible blindness," as dyslexia arguably was prior to its legitimization in recent decades, developmental prosopagnosia requires that the individual navigate the typical social networks—from the playgroups of childhood to extended family units, to the school environment to the community and later professional arenas—with face recognition skills that are less reliable in offering relevant identity information. Given this, the child learns to cope, subconsciously (or perhaps consciously at times), developing strategies for identifying others and dealing with the challenges—unrecognized though they may be—of living with prosopagnosia.

## ACQUIRED PROSOPAGNOSIA

> Well, there's this tall, short, skinny, fat, blonde, brunette, redhead who's very graceful in a confusing sort of way. (Jim Cooke, age 63, acquired prosopagnosia at age 49)

Jim Cooke, the acquired prosopagnosic quoted earlier, speaks with a gravelly voice, his New York accent as strong as his New York wit. He has a tendency to laugh often, "rib" relentlessly, and offer a compassionate ear. Normally sighted for 49 years, Jim became prosopagnosic following rare, life-saving brain surgery. Unable to recognize faces ever since, Jim has been interviewed for British and Japanese television and also gives a lecture every year at a local optometry program.

He was on the telephone one day, describing his search for a neurologist who could help him to identify the problem with "seeing" that he was having after the surgery. He explained that he searched hard until he found someone exceptional:

> …I got an appointment… I saw him [and told him that] I don't recognize…my reflection in the mirror… I look in the mirror, I have to search around to see my reflection.

Here Jim was emphatic:

> I don't see me there…and he [the neurologist] held up one finger, "Just a moment," walked over to his floor to ceiling bookcase, scanned the titles, pulled a book out, turned to something ridiculous like page 713, xeroxed a page, got out his highlighter and he highlighted…visual

agnosia, prosopagnosia, and the face in the looking glass syndrome, taken from the writings of Oscar Wilde, because quite often, but not always, people with prosopagnosia either don't see themselves... He told me that that's what it sounded like the problem was, and then I put it together and realized his diagnosis was right on the button...

Forty-nine years "face sighted," Jim had a job as owner of a wholesale jewelry business. In a crowd of thousands, he could recognize one customer from the previous year who had bought hundreds of a particular style of necklace from him: that knowledge enabled him to zero in on that customer when she browsed at his table. Yet following brain surgery some years ago, he suddenly failed to recognize even his own teenage kids.

In terms of the challenges of face recognition deficit, the point of comparison that Jim offers is enlightening to those seeking to comprehend prosopagnosia. Describing how it felt to him to go from a life of face recognition to that of one who could no longer recognize faces, Jim responded:

> Mmmm... It's almost as though you're at a costume party... You're at a fancy costume party, everybody is wearing a mask except for you. And you know some of the people at the party, but you don't know everybody...at the party, and so some people walk past you and don't say "Hi," and some people walk past you and say "Hi, Jim"...but you don't know who anybody is and you don't know which people are there that you do know and which ones you don't so the whole world is wearing masks except for you...

In fact, after spending a great deal of time trying to decide how to describe his case of acquired prosopagnosia to a local optometry school audience at which he gives an annual talk, Jim decided to provide the students with a print-out including the following words: "that that is is that that is not is not."

Later, he explained to the audience that these are simply words without meaning:

> And tell them just look at the words...they know what each word means, but what does the entire piece of paper mean? That's sort of me looking at a face. I see the face and see the eyes...but it doesn't mean anything if you're looking at words. Until you put some punctuation in. Then it has perfect meaning. What it says is, "That that is, is. Period. That that is not, is not. Period." But without the punctuation, it's just a bunch of words. I look at a face, it's just a bunch of features, means nothing. So it's almost as though the punctuation is missing when I look at a face.

## THEORY OF PSYCHOSOCIAL PATTERNS OF COPING

The prosopagnosic woman smiles graciously, talks with those at the party, some whom she knows, others whom she does not recognize by looking at their faces. Within moments, she will hear their voices, glean identity from words, and depending upon her social skills, she may even know just what kind of information to offer without revealing her lack of identity information, as she seeks to determine their identity. She is someone who has thrived, a professional who comprehends the social world. How is her experience with prosopagnosia, which she has had from childhood, different from that of Jim, who has by now been prosopagnosic for more than a decade but grown accustomed to his loss of face recognition skills?

Table 1.1 describes a theory of psychosocial differences.

Regardless of the kind of prosopagnosia, the individual with face recognition deficit is usually able to see and point to the eyes, nose, and mouth, as well as to other parts of the face. In fact, her ability to do so may cause others—even the prosopagnosic herself—to erroneously conclude that she is discerning identity via normal face processing skills, despite her actually using non-facial recognition strategies for determining who others are.

In some ways, perhaps, the experiences of the acquired prosopagnosic parallel those of individuals congenitally blind—that is, those born blind—versus those adventitiously blind—that is, those who have gone blind. It is important to comprehend that unlike Jim, who experienced a sense of loss when he acquired prosopagnosia, the developmental prosopagnosic does not experience the absence of an ability with which she had been familiar.

While the experiences of individual prosopagnosics may vary widely and will not fit neatly into a chart, it is useful to consider some of the psychosocial differences that appear to emerge between the two groups, as described in Table 1.1. Regardless of the kind of prosopagnosia, finding ways in which to bolster the individual's ability to effectively navigate the social realm is important. Having insight into the challenges of developmental prosopagnosic will be important.

Prosopagnosics can be found in many kinds of professions. They may be academics, engineers, educators, clerks, artists, and more. At least one research study on the topic (Zhu et al. 2009) has found no relationship between face recognition deficit and IQ. Regardless of the type of prosopagnosia, the issue of face recognition deficit will pervade many aspects of the individual's life. Some people are able to thrive socially and an intervention, likely to disrupt growth, is not recommended for them. Others, however, may benefit from specific strategies for inclusion. In such cases, disruptions caused by the deficit should be minimized, while those adults providing

## Table 1.1 Developmental versus acquired prosopagnosia

| Acquired Prosopagnosia | Developmental Prosopagnosia |
| --- | --- |
| Acquired prosopagnosia is a face recognition deficit that occurs as a result of brain trauma such as that caused by a car accident, brain surgery, or stroke. | Developmental prosopagnosia occurs from childhood. The individual grows up adapting to life with highly limited face recognition ability. |
| Acquired prosopagnosics and their supporters reach a point of comparison that helps the prosopagnosic herself, as well as members of the community, to comprehend her impairment; this understanding may lead to others' providing the prosopagnosic with identity information. | The individual may be unaware that the visual identity information available to her is far less adequate than that to which most others have access. She may go for years unaware that her face perception ability it truly limited, in comparison with others. this lack of identity information may lead to social errors or (for some prosopagnosics) some social risk-taking, when identity is uncertain. |
| When Jim had major brain surgery, which had an impact on his face recognition ability and some physical coordination, this became immediately obvious to others, who provided support by offering him the information that he needed regarding identity, when they remembered to do so. He also seemed comfortable with asking for that information. | The individual needs to learn to minimize the number of identity mistakes that will occur and to cope with them effectively when they do happen, so as to minimize the potential negative repercussions. |
| While some research has found the ability to process emotional facial expressions to be impaired among acquired prosopagnosics, there are also studies that have found the ability to be intact. Acquired prosopagnosia, by definition, occurs in response to physical trauma. Given this, there may be other physical challenges with which the individual needs to cope. For example, in addition to prosopagnosia, Jim also has apraxia, a loss of some physical coordination for certain skills, such as buttoning a shirt. | Developmental prosopagnosics may be unaware that the way in which they see faces is vastly different from the manner in which most people do. We often talk about *what* we see; it is less usual for us to discuss *how* we see. Given the tendency for facial features and the topic of recognition itself to go undiscussed, it is currently common for developmental prosopagnosia to go undiagnosed. In terms of development, what begins as a physiological challenge for the child (that is, cognitive issues related to facial processing) can become a psychosocial one, as she gradually adapts (or maladapts) to the deficit. |
| Some acquired prosopagnosics experience crisis following the loss of an important, familiar life skill that they have always known. There may also be an "aha" moment, as Jim demonstrated in the previous section when he described the importance of finding a neurologist who could help him to pinpoint how his visual processing had changed. Although his neurologist did not "cure" the prosopagnosia, it appears that the doctor's naming it brought Jim some relief. He had a "handle" on his issue, so that he could begin to address it. | For developmental prosopagnosics, the ability to discern facial expressions is separate from that of processing faces. As will be discussed in greater depth later in the book, while some developmental prosopagnosics can perceive facial expressions well, others are partly or severely limited in this area of understanding. |
| | There may for some be critically difficult moments of non-recognition or even the mourning for a life skill that the prosopagnosic has never had, once she discovers that she has the deficit, but there can also be an "aha" moment, as in the case of acquired prosopagnosia, an appreciation for having a name for the recognition problem, which can lead to steps to understand and navigate around it. |

support in a child's life find vehicles for tapping and maximizing areas of talent.

Whether an individual has acquired or developmental prosopagnosia, there appear to be benefits in having a name for the cognitive visual deficit. Identifying a cognovisual obstacle can lead to a prosopagnosic's developing effective strategies to glean missing information.

## THE SOCIALLY THRIVING CHILD

As has already been mentioned, while some developmental prosopagnosics have friends and enjoy their interactions with others, there are those with face recognition deficit who experience significant social challenge, and these are the children for whom these chapters are written. Which factors separate those who thrive socially from those who flounder because of the deficit is a question for further research. One wonders whether those with prosopagnosia who lack access to some or many of the broad range of emotional expressions may face greater social challenge, because even such inclusive acts as an expression of recognition, which normally precedes greeting a recognized person (what may be called the "hello look") may enable some with prosopagnosia—namely children who recognize emotional expressions—to carry on appropriate conversations that ultimately lead to opportunities to glean identity information, recognize others, and maintain friendships. For example, such hints as voice, conversation habits, and gestures offered in response to a greeting (that had been offered in response to the "hello look") can lead to important information. Indeed, some developmental prosopagnosics say that if someone says "hello" to them, seemingly out of the blue, it can be a startling experience because they feel that they lack warning that they are about to be spoken to. And while some developmental prosopagnosics perceive emotional expressions well, others have difficulty with comprehending some or many of the broad spectrum of expressions so important to communication.

Whether the child's natural character, encouragement from adults to take social risks, or being placed in situations in which she will be able to succeed will contribute to her ability to thrive socially is another question worthy of exploration. In some contexts, it is unsafe for a child to say hello to an unknown person. However, if the child fails to greet friends in new contexts, she may inadvertently offend them, and the challenge of maintaining friendships, given such circumstances, may present her with a difficult dilemma (even when she is unaware that she is ignoring "known" individuals). In addition, some members of the community may attribute the child's failure to recognize friends to inattention or lack of caring or effort, which can, in turn, contribute to social distance that reduces the number of invitations and opportunities for social development.

Furthermore, given that a percentage of prosopagnosics lack access to the full range of facial expressions, some children may be missing an aspect of language as important to communication as words themselves: the subtexts, the parenthetical non-verbal aspects of communication that can confirm or refute the words that a speaker is saying.

## CHILDHOOD-ACQUIRED PROSOPAGNOSIA

For the purpose of this book, cases of those who have had a known physical abnormality, whether brain trauma or eye disease such as congenital cataract, which could disrupt visual development during the apparently critical learning period for faces, will be separated from those in which no known physical disruption has occurred. The term "childhood-acquired prosopagnosia," will be used to describe those cases of face recognition deficit that apparently occur in response to a known physical event.

Glenn Alperin, one of the interviewees for this book, has been for years a kind of leader in advocating for the general public's understanding of face recognition deficit. His perspective is quite rare in that he and his parents were aware of his facial recognition challenges from the time of his childhood. A very thoughtful individual, he has been interviewed for *CNN*, *The Boston Globe*, and other media outlets regarding his views on prosopagnosia.

Glenn suffered a fall from a crib at 16 months of age and was consequently comatose for 6 weeks. He explains how, when he emerged from the coma, his parents noticed that he had an unusual facial recognition problem:

> I know that based on what I've been told, I was a very fast walker, a very fast talker. After the accident, I essentially had to learn it all over again…when I came out of the coma, I would be crawling around for a few seconds, actually beginning to walk again… It was almost like watching….tv… a fast-forward camera mechanism, the way my mom described it to me.

> One thing that my mom tells me that I did a lot [following this fall] when I was a child was… I would ask questions like, "Are you my mommy? Are you my daddy?" It's not just usually a young child's question, because your average child knows who the mommy and the daddy really is. (Glenn Alperin, childhood-acquired prosopagnosia)

## Early visual deprivation

There is an additional group of children who appear to have difficulties with face recognition. As important research at McMaster University, Canada, has revealed (Grand, Mondloch, Maurer and Brent 2004), infants who have had congenital cataract surgeries between 3.2 and 6.2 months have been shown in studies years later to have developed impaired facial processing, even if visual acuity in one eye (the one without the cataract) is normal. There may be a critical period during which face recognition ability normally develops, if infants are exposed to the opportunities that they need to develop visually.

## How prosopagnosia manifests

### COMPOSITES BASED UPON VARIOUS INTERVIEWS

#### THE CASE OF ROB, DEVELOPMENTAL PROSOPAGNOSIA

Rob, age ten, gets a ride to school with his mother at 7:00 am, and entering the schoolyard he finds there is no-one that he immediately recognizes. However, one boy, Jimmy, a Caucasian child—and one of the few whose mother lets him wear an earring in his left ear—is familiar to Rob, who runs to Jimmy. The two play together on the jungle gym before the school bell rings and all the children are required to line up.

A group of brown-haired boys are pushing each other in line and someone shoves Rob who responds by pushing back. There is a jumble of children, a rearrangement of people in line. A teacher arrives in response to the hubbub and, on hearing the story, inquires, "Rob, who pushed you?" Rob looks at the sea of faces and responds, "I don't know."

Rob loves homeroom. Although unaware as to the reason for his comfort, he experiences a feeling of relief in homeroom. The desks are arranged in order, into small groups, and everyone sits at the same desk every day. Each child has a name sign on their desk that they had made on the first day of school, and Rob feels right "at home." However, art class is a different story. Everyone walks around that class, and sits in a different seat every day. And Rob has a problem with the fact that there are three boys in that class who look somewhat alike. They all have short, brown hair, and one of them—Rob is uncertain as to which—was responsible for having pushed him earlier in the day. Unwilling to risk a confrontation, Rob avoids all three of the boys who have short brown hair. However, there is a sweet African American girl, Martha, with whom Rob often works during art class. He knows her well and can easily find her when children are choosing materials and desks because she has long cornbraids that distinguish her from the other African American children in the room.

After school, Rob usually walks three blocks to the pharmacy at which his mother works, so that they can ride home together. Rob does not recognize some emotional expressions and he is often surprised when some of the other children say "hello" to him as they pass, because he does not know who they are... To put it simply, he doesn't recognize the "hello look," that facial expression that people subconsciously form once they have recognized an individual, and that offers warning that the individual is about to say hello. Rather than smile, Rob, startled, grimaces a bit, but he does say hello back to them. Rob's mother has warned him not to talk to strangers—but, with a few exceptions, just about everybody is a stranger. And Rob walks quietly to meet his mother.

One day, Rob's mother hears about prosopagnosia through a friend of a friend. She hears that some (not all) prosopagnosic children are somewhat isolated and she asks, "Rob, can you see faces?" Annoyed, he responds, "Yes, I can." [What a ridiculous question. He can point to eyes, nose, and mouth. He could do that since he was a baby. This is insulting.] When she inquires, "Do you think that some of your loneliness is related to your not recognizing people?" Rob responds, "I recognize people." After all, he recognizes his mother, teacher, Jimmy, Martha, and some others. In fact, as far as he is concerned, his face recognition skills are "normal"; everyone else recognizes as he does. His mother turns away and prepares dinner, satisfied that they have had this discussion.

Indeed, Rob's mother, herself, may also be prosopagnosic, because there appears to be a genetic component, and she could view his skills as normal—even if she knew about them in great detail.

## THE CASE OF STEVE, AGE 70, ACQUIRED PROSOPAGNOSIA

Steve had a stroke three weeks ago, and he is coping with some significant issues, including memory issues. Something, [in addition to what he had discussed with his doctor,] *feels* different to Steve, but he can't put a finger on it. The many doctors in white coats and nurses who have come to see him have told him that he would have some cognitive difficulties, and he does feel a bit strange.

One day, he is in a department store, when a woman he has just passed in the hardware aisle says, "Hi, Steve." It now clicks. He recognizes her voice: it's Marge, the woman who has been living next door to him for the past 20 years. Steve is shocked, because he now realizes that he had not recognized her. He *never* would have failed to recognize Marge before the stroke.

Steve talks with family and friends, and word gets out that he no longer recognizes faces. When he goes to a party with many of his old friends, several come up to him and introduce themselves: "Hi, Steve, it's me, Dan. So sorry about your stroke. Hey, we should play some tennis if you're up for it at some point." "Hi, Steve, it's Janet. How ya been?" Steve has some difficulty adapting, particularly at first, but with strength and persistence, he does adapt—and realizes that there are many things that he still *can* do. And he has the support of his community along the way.

*Please note: These examples are provided as case studies based upon anecdotal evidence, interviews, etc. Every prosopagnosic's experience is different, and certainly there are also those who love and have a very positive social experience in school.

# Chapter 2

# SEEING FACES

I have two children. I will tell you about looking into the face of my first child, Ellie. Several hours after she was born, they placed her in my arms. She looked into my eyes with a deep, knowing look. She knew I was her mother. With her very dark blue eyes, she looked into my soul. When I looked into her eyes, I felt as though we had known each other forever. (Jenni Welch, normally face sighted)

Face perception is integral to human relationships, beginning with the most basic mother–child bond and expanding outward to the social networks that we navigate in our lives. Above, Jenni's looking into, "knowing" her daughter's face, while only one aspect of what must be a complex bond, is part of the connection that she feels. When one considers the early emergence of skills normally associated with recognizing faces, the social challenge to the prosopagnosic becomes more apparent.

The research suggests that newborns prefer looking at faces or face-like structures (Goren *et al.* 1975; Mondloch *et al.* 1999), and that the child focuses upon his visual surroundings at a distance that in some studies has ranged from 7.5 inches (19 centimetres) and in others to 9.84 inches (25 centimetres) (Haynes, White and Held 1965) and which is said to increase as the child's visual system develops (Brookman 1983 as in Aslin; Braddick *et al.* 1979). As has been observed, the ability to accommodate—to visually focus—at this distance will enable a baby to focus upon his mother's face while nursing (Karmiloff and Karmiloff-Smith 1998). The intensity of light must be significantly higher for most children to be able to perceive light at all, for the still immature visual system continues to develop (Mondloch *et al.* 1999). The visual acuity of an infant has been suggested to be 40 times lower than that of an adult.

The question of whether face perception is typically inborn, learned, or both is yet to be determined (Gauthier and Nelson 2001), and recent studies will need to be further probed, replicated, or refuted as we continue to explore the evolution of face recognition ability.

There have been studies that probe the question of how and whether babies can perceive faces, and a challenge in devising experiments is that one might be able to determine what a newborn gazes at, but it is more difficult to explore the question of *how* the child sees. One experiment, for example, aimed to determine which aspect of the mother's face the baby could see (Pascalis *et al.* 1995), while another found that newborns prefer looking at the faces of their mothers to viewing those of strangers (Bushnell 2001). In the former study, scientists measured infant gaze when the babies' mothers appeared to their children in scarves or bathing caps and found that when the boundaries of the mothers' faces were hidden, the infants did not recognize their mothers' faces (Pascalis *et al.* 1995). Apparently, infants are better at recognizing the outline shape of the face and hair—and not the face itself. It is interesting to note that (as will be discussed in greater detail later in the book), some prosopagnosics, too, use the shape of the border between face and hair as well as the characteristics of the hair with which to recognize people.

The ability to discern and then comprehend facial expressions begins in infancy (Nelson 1987), and there is research to suggest that the child is able to perceive a difference between happy and sad facial expressions by three months (Barrera and Maurer 1981). In fact, he actually does better at distinguishing the difference between them, according to the research, if it is a "caretaker"—someone familiar—at whom he is looking. Over time, the growing child will also come to discriminate between expressions of anger, fear, surprise, disgust and others. Between three and seven months, a child is usually able to distinguish between happy and fearful facial expressions. By approximately the second or third month, infants can usually accomplish the "social smile," which involves seeing another's smile and reciprocating it. A study of seven-month-old infants suggests that the clue of "motion" is crucial to the infant's recognizing expressions.

One's ability to interpret and comprehend emotional facial expressions is by no means perfect into adulthood, and some adults continue to have difficulty with discerning emotional facial expressions even though the expressions are, for the most part, universal across cultures. Indeed, research probing the impact of the individual's initial state, gender, age, personal history, and more, when interpreting emotional expressions are currently taking place in laboratories across the world.

Certain abilities related to the development of face recognition skills, such as a child's perception of visual motion, begin in early infancy. Indeed, intriguingly, this is an ability that even those who are blind from early childhood and have sight-enabling surgeries years later have been found to possess. As vision, in general, and face recognition, in particular, continue to evolve, a child experiences a series of changes that exhibit an ingenious evolution, enabling him to gently, gradually, prepare for and adjust to visual change. Tears form to reflect emotion, enabling a baby to communicate need, albeit subconsciously. A child can see objects that exhibit sharp contrast, perceive black and white images, and, with time, see a difference between red and green. There is evidence that yellow and blue are distinguishable during the third and fourth months of life, as the immature retina continues to develop and the dimmer world becomes more vivid.

Scientists examining infant gaze or measuring brain activity in order to "gain insight into" children's perceptive skills have hypothesized that holistic face processing is detectable by approximately the fourth to fifth month (Fagan 1972; Otsuka *et al.* 2007; Rose *et al.* 2008). As described in the discussion of prosopagnosia in Chapter 1, some scientists assert that those presented with a picture of an inverted face need to mentally invert the face to comprehend it; those who see the face "holistically," as inseparable features, will take more time and have greater difficulty with the task than those who mentally invert the face a part at a time. This hypothesis has been used by some researchers to explain "the inversion effect" that children experience. And by six months most children can recognize their caregiver's face. An infant's facial perception skills are relatively broad at around six months, because children can recognize the faces of humans and of animals of other species, such as monkeys, at about that time (Pascals, Haan and Nelson 2002). Approximately three months later (at about nine months of age), that skill "narrows" so that the infant can recognize only human faces.

Eventually, a child develops the ability to discern gender from faces, and there is evidence that an infant can match some of the gender-based characteristics of voice and face by eight months. He can perform tasks that enable him to socialize—for example, he can follow the direction of another's gaze.

The ability for a child to recognize his own image in the mirror is thought to develop between 15 and 24 months. This is demonstrated through an experiment involving placing a dot on a child's forehead (Anderson 2004). The child then looks in the mirror and, if he realizes that the dot is on his own forehead, then he will probably try to touch it; this demonstrates that he recognizes his reflection. One should consider, however, that a child of this age may be able to perform some self-recognition tasks without facial recognition skills, because it is possible to recognize the other parts of one's body and to identify, for example, motion and gesture, without recognizing one's face per se. Indeed, some research (Bertenthal and Fischer 1978) has suggested that self-recognition does not involve one task, a skill which one is "suddenly" able to perform, but rather describes a series of stages through which an individual passes on the way to typical self-recognition.

Indeed, this skill of face perception, of which most are unaware, is one that will extend to virtually every human relationship that an infant, then growing child, and adult will have. The complex skills involved in face recognition enable humans to identify others, comprehend social networks, accomplish goals, and develop sophisticated understanding.

Donna Peterson, our developmental prosopagnosic from Chapter 1, is a mother, like Jenni quoted at the beginning of this chapter. She was asked what she remembered seeing when she first held her children in her arms.

[Question: "Do you remember what your children's faces looked like when they were born?"]

> The truth? No. [*Describing one child*] I remember she was small, and I remember she had a widow's peak [a triangular wisp of hair at the forehead], because when I touched her head, I remember touching her widow's peak up front. Most of the time, her eyes were like closed. They opened every so often when she was hungry, and she used to cry.

Donna's description seemed to focus upon the size of the face, rather than a draw to its features:

> Well, I saw her face was, it was a little, tiny face. And she was very soft and cuddly and ah I always had her wrapped in a blanket, in a nightgown that tied on the bottom, and then I put a blanket on top and wrapped around her, because she was so small. She was a small, little baby. And when I came home, everybody jumped and tried to grab her! Everybody wanted to hold her and grab her, "Oh, I want to hold her, I want to hold her, I want to hold her!"

Describing another daughter, who was initially put in an oxygen tent following birth, Donna explained:

> Well, I saw a little girl, she had a little bit of dark hair… I put my hand on her stomach to feel her heartbeat. Then her little toes were sticking out at the end, and I would take each…and rub each foot a little. Her hands were clenched, and the only way she could tell it was me was because I put my finger, I clenched my finger in her hand, so she knew it was her mother.

[Question: When you held her in your arms…?]

> She looked beautiful. She was breathing well. She looked good. And
> her lungs were fabulous: she knew how to cry…

Face recognition and the ability to perceive expressions will offer most infants and children a skill that will gradually enable them to respond to those in their lives through an unspoken language shared across cultures and global boundaries. An infant will access information that will enable him to share joy, comfort sorrow, modify his behavior if he is doing something with which another is displeased, and to continue activities that bring others pleasure. Prosopagnosic or not, whatever we see and remember will become not only the world around us, but also the world within us. It will enable our mental representations, guide our decision making, and form the architecture of our imagination, comprising the very real and perceived events—within and without—that make us human. Whatever one's perception, the exciting opportunity for comprehending perception itself, and tapping talent, is significant. As Lydia, who perceives faces normally, was asked, "Do you have a child? If so, do you remember what it felt like to look into that child's eyes when the child was an infant?" She replied as follows:

> I remember the first thing I thought was: "Oh, so this is what she looks
> like, finally!" Then I looked for my own features in hers. She had my
> eyes, and my mouth, in the shapes and colors, except her lips were
> very pink. She had a chin shaped like my husband's sister and mother.
> Her features were very symmetrical. I can still remember her facial
> features and how they have changed. She now has more oval-shaped
> eyes, rather than the rounded shape that was dominant when she was
> an infant. Her nose is less round, more elongated. Her chin has stayed
> the same. (*Lydia Mathers, normally face sighted*)

Lydia's ability to recognize her child, to comprehend the baby's face, is one that will color their relationship in the years to come.

Certainly, our current understanding of the prevalence of prosopagnosia drives home the fact that face recognition involves an intricate series of processes that is more fragile than had been considered as recently as a decade ago. As one considers the normal early emergence of face recognition ability, it becomes clear that the prosopagnosic may face a significant challenge in obtaining identity information and finding ways in which to help others to understand his needs, whether or not he chooses to disclose the prosopagnosia. Not only will this challenge to others' understanding require effective communication and/or strategies (particularly if the prosopagnosic doesn't disclose the deficit), it will also require a leap in empathy on the part of members of the community, who will need to comprehend that an individual can perceive in a way that is quite different from the way in which they themselves have done from childhood, even if this difference is not visually apparent.

Chapter 3

# BENEFITS TO CHILDREN OF FACE RECOGNITION

There are many ways in which face recognition helps a child to develop, and it is challenging to tease apart how this skill contributes to normal development. As one considers the ways in which to offer a child with face recognition deficit the right amount of social support so as to promote inclusion while nurturing talent in other areas, it is worthwhile to explore how recognizing faces can have an impact on development.

Abraham Maslow's (1943) humanistic theory of psychology provides a lens through which we may view the benefits of face recognition and begin to consider the ways in which prosopagnosia has an impact on a growing child. Such a framework is useful as we arrive at strategies for supporting a child with face recognition deficit who passes through various stages toward becoming a healthy, fulfilled human being. Maslow explained that a child, teen, and then adult climbs a hierarchical ladder of needs and, in so doing, develops toward general physical and emotional health and well-being. Let's apply this theory as we examine the benefits of normal face recognition skills.

## MASLOW'S STAGES
### Physiological
According to Maslow, all humans should have their physiological needs of food, water, air to breathe, etc. met before moving on to higher developmental stages.

As a child begins the process of learning to recognize faces during infancy, physiological needs are met, and the evolution of face recognition skills begins to contribute to physical and emotional well-being. As discussed in Chapter 2, studies reveal that even as early as infancy the child is beginning to recognize the emotional expressions of her caregiver's face. Perhaps a sense of security evolves as the child comes to recognize that the caregiver is, for example, pleased. The child will be able to learn what to do, which behaviors are acceptable and which to avoid as she grows. Emotional communication via facial expressions occurs as the child is able to master the social smile—one that reciprocates another's — at approximately two to three months (Connolly 2010).

## Safety

Safety needs must be met in order for the growing child to move toward fulfilling other, more advanced psychosocial needs.

Most sighted children can recognize a parent or caregiver by six months, and that adult will usually be protective of the child versus a stranger, thus contributing to both physical and emotional security. Indeed, throughout childhood and adult life, recognizing faces can contribute to the individual's physical and emotional well-being. One should consider that the child may be able to recognize the caregiver using the other senses or even by making use of other, non-facial aspects of vision. However, these strategies may take longer or be somewhat less reliable than face recognition. Recognizing faces not only helps the child know to whom she should run for safety—but also, whom to avoid. This may at times include potentially physically threatening individuals.

## Social (love, belonging)

The child forms close bonds with others as she develops the ability to navigate social relationships, to find her place among others. Regardless of sensory strength and weaknesses, it is important to identify others, whether by face recognition or some other means, in order to gather the information required to connect with them, and eventually to navigate complex social networks. Recognition skills can help the individual in the quest toward building meaningful relationships in school, community, and, eventually, in the workplace.

## Self-esteem

The child should have a positive sense of self, and this involves opportunities to explore and develop talent, to be appreciated for contributions. It is also crucial to learn how to accomplish daily tasks effectively and to find ways to meet others' expectations, to be respected. Feeling a sense of competence in doing so is important, and finding ways in which to cope with identity errors is crucial. When one considers the possible repercussions of untimely social mistakes, one understands the importance of learning to deal in a healthy manner with the potential for embarrassment that is sometimes associated with prosopagnosia.

## Self-actualization

The individual needs to discover, express and contribute to society in ways personally meaningful and socially relevant.

Finding ways to navigate around prosopagnosia, to cope with it in a healthy manner, is important to a child's thriving.

What are some ways of improving the prosopagnosic child's sense of safety, while encouraging her independence? What can be done to contribute to the child's sense of love and belonging within the community, even though she lacks the ability to visually recognize some or all of the people within that community? What kinds of strategies will help her to successfully navigate the social realm, so as to build self-esteem, while also developing talent in other areas?

The following chapters of this book, which offer tips for supporting the prosopagnosic child can address strategies for meeting her needs. In so doing, it is useful to consider Maslow's framework in determining whether there are ways to help support the child as she strives at each stage in the journey.

Chapter 4

# FACES, MATH AND MOTION: THE CLUSTERING OF TALENT AND IMPAIRMENT AREAS

## AUTISM AND ASPERGER SYNDROME

Parents of children who deal with special challenges such as autism or Asperger syndrome may understandably feel that they have a "full plate" and need to be selective regarding issues for which to provide support. It can be extremely helpful to tease apart those areas that will enable a child to socialize more effectively, and identifying the problem needs to be one of the first steps. It has not been demonstrated that all children on the autistic spectrum have prosopagnosia. Indeed, not all prosopagnosics are on the autistic spectrum. Yet, anecdotally and research supported, there appears to be a correlation between prosopagnosia and those children on the spectrum, as some have already noted (Klin *et al.* 1999; Pietz, Ebinger and Rating 2003; Grandin 2006). Comprehending prosopagnosia in isolation is useful to understanding the child's challenges and may make offering support for the "social piece" a more manageable task.

### Motion and autism

Some autistic people say that they don't like to look at faces because of the uncomfortable way in which faces move, according to Temple Grandin (2006), whose brilliant book, *Thinking in Pictures*, describes her life with autism. And while some autistics find motion—particularly that which comes from eye contact—to be repelling, others, such as Grandin herself, have described it as "stimulating" (p.69). Indeed, Grandin stated that she was fascinated by the motion of objects such as kites and airplanes during childhood.

Motion is processed atypically by autistic people, according to research studies on the topic (Milne *et al.* 2006; Vandenbrouke *et al.* 2008), and studies in perception related to dyslexia (Stein 2003), for example, suggest that motion plays a role in cognition.

Faces are patterns in motion. As the parts of the face express and move, and heads turn, there is constant movement of which one has to keep track. It would make sense that individuals highly sensitive or otherwise atypical in terms of motional perception would find interactions involving faces to be daunting—perhaps at times, for some, repelling—with images difficult to comprehend. Eyelids open and close vertically, eyeballs move in multiple directions, lips pucker, purse, pout, open, close, grin, smile, smirk. Cheeks expand, faces lengthen, eyebrows rise—and lower again. And sometimes many of these happen at once. For a person highly sensitive to motion, the perception of facial motion can be difficult. It makes sense that autistic people, who have been found to perceive motion atypically, often find perceiving faces to be daunting.

Anecdotally, it has been noted that face recognition deficit also often accompanies atypical perception of math and topography—navigation skills—and it is worth considering whether the same atypical motional perception that interferes with "face sight," if you will, also influences other areas of cognition, in some cases enabling (or disrupting) talent. That is, while faces are visual patterns in motion, math is also patterns in motion—patterns of objects or numbers in motion through cognitive space. Facility with math requires an ability to mentally move patterns, to make the patterns of numbers (or numbers of objects or in some cases, letters) interact. And the ability to navigate (that is, sense of direction), topographical ability, is based upon an ability to anchor point A, to hold it in place, and to comprehend the motional patterns that take us from A to B.

For all of these capabilities, one needs to hang onto a mental image, fix it in place, and with facility set in action the patterns, synthesize them, comprehend them. If one perceived motion atypically, then it would make sense that not only would face perception be atypical, but also other areas in which mentally representing and moving patterns occurs would be atypical, too. An overly sensitive perception of motion could impair seeing the patterns of faces—but also contribute to facility in math, for example. This may account for the clustering of talent—or impairment—in these areas among prosopagnosics. That is, while authors such as Temple Grandin have noted the high ability of autistics (who are often prosopagnosic) to comprehend spatial relations, others have noted anecdotally that some prosopagnosics have topographical agnosia and math difficulty. This relationship between face perception, navigation ability, and math can be called "photomotion."

The patterns of numbers known as math need to move, to be cognitively manipulated, for problems to be solved. In fact, the perception of motion enables humans to mentally manipulate symbols, in general, whether these symbols be those of visual numbers as they are tracked in multiple directions in our Arabic math notational system, the change in the shape of a mouth to a smile (a social symbol necessary for developing social understanding), or difference in the shade of color from mauve to violet, a leap in sound from a high pitch to a lower one (to express a serious or sad tone, for example), or the motion needed to move from one letter to the next in reading. The perception of motion will ultimately influence what will be understood and what will become available in memory, with potential to evolve into talent—and even learning style. And I believe that it is this relativity of motional perception that contributes to the diversity of face perception and ultimately, as varied notational systems become accessible, determining learning styles. To be clear, it appears that the same atypical perception of motion that leads to impairment in some areas, such as faces, contributes to talent (or impairment) in others. It is interesting that those with prosopagnosia have been found to exhibit spatial genius in some cases and topographical agnosia—impairment in this area—in others.

## THE CASE OF NORBERT WEINER

Keith Devlin, in his wonderful book, *The Math Gene: How Mathematical Thinking Evolved and Why Numbers are Like Gossip* (2001), described a story of Norbert Weiner, a famous, apparently prosopagnosic mathematician from the Massachusetts Institute of Technology, who started the cybernetics field and also contributed significantly to that of electrical engineering. Weiner, who was Swedish-born and moved to the US, where he pursued his work and eventually raised a family in Massachusetts, was supposed to finish work one day and then return to the new house that his family had just purchased. However, out of habit, he arrived at his old house, where he saw a little girl sitting out in front of the house. As Devlin tells the story, Weiner had apparently forgotten his new address and asked the child as to where the previous owners had moved. The girl turned out to be Weiner's daughter, whom he hadn't recognized, and who explained smilingly that her mother, who had cleverly anticipated Daddy's mistake, had asked the daughter to go and get him (p.130).

When one sees, it is usually with little awareness of all that the visual system accomplishes in processing motion, but the extraordinary task of making sense of an apparently moving world takes place for sighted people with each glance, daily. The feat of identifying one's visual surroundings, despite the need to reconcile these motional patterns, is accomplished, enabling us to literally make sense of the world.

Those film projectors, from the days when movie films were common, sometimes showed scenes that were too fast during start-up. Images would come across the screen so rapidly at times that viewers failed to comprehend what was being shown. However, if the film were slowed down, one could recognize, for example, that it was a film about three people, of three different races, who had just arrived in a city. It took slowing down the motion of these events to a speed perceptible to the viewer for the movie to become comprehensible. In fact, in real life, even when a person appears stationary, it is necessary to reconcile motion as the eyes move—in order to identify the events of the world and objects that comprise it. This is discussed further in "Resolution theory" (Mindick 2005a), part of which is further described in the Appendix of this book.

Chapter 5

# RECOGNIZING NON-RECOGNITION

While on the one hand it is important to avoid causing a problem where there is none, because some prosopagnosic children thrive extremely well academically and socially, others do need help. Ignoring the issue in the case of a child who is isolated as a result of the deficit is simply unfair. It is one thing to accept the child for who she is; not everyone is meant to be a social butterfly. The child may have rich depth and a profound capacity for meaningful friendships, in addition to talent in many areas, while choosing to be a person who mostly enjoys solitude. However, solitude should be a choice—and not the result of social isolation or underdeveloped social skills related to the prosopagnosia. Family members, educators, psychologists, and members of the community need to be smart, aware, and compassionate, in terms of determining whether or not the child has prosopagnosia—and, if so, whether it needs to be addressed and how.

Given the current lack of regular testing for children, combined with their generally limited understanding of how their face recognition skills compare with those of others, it is useful to have some "tip of the iceberg" ideas for recognizing prosopagnosia in childhood. You should not simply ask a child, "Do you recognize faces?" in order to obtain an answer. While none of the points listed below will definitively determine that a child has face recognition deficit, here are a few common clues:

- Does the child...
    - know the names of only a few students in class, and generally avoid calling people by name? Is there an extreme reluctance to join groups? Although this may simply be related to shyness, it could also be a sign of wishing to avoid mingling with people whom one has difficulty recognizing

- o have trouble recognizing an individual whom she knows well and frequently sees, if that person is wearing a head covering or new hairstyle or is seen in a new context?

- o become confused in following movie plots when the main characters have similar build, hair coloring and length, and wear similar clothing or uniforms?

- o fail to say hello in some contexts, yet act friendly in others? Consistently?

- o have trouble recognizing photos of familiar people in unfamiliar clothes and atypical contexts? It is important to be cautious here. Sometimes context clues help a child a great deal. Recognizing Aunt Maggie in a photo taken during a New Hampshire trip does not mean that the child is using a facial clue

- o have trouble recognizing famous people to whom she has been regularly exposed via the newspapers or TV?

- Do most of her friends dress unusually or have visual traits that would make them distinguishable to a prosopagnosic? Many children have friends who dress unusually. However, if a child seems to recognize only people who dress unusually or who have a distinguishing characteristic (e.g. the only curly-headed boy or very tall girl in the class, or one from a different race from the majority of the other children), this may be related to prosopagnosia.

- Is the child on the autistic spectrum? Although not all people with prosopagnosia have autism or Asperger syndrome, prosopagnosia does appear to be prevalent within that population.

Many childcare professionals who are practicing today have probably spent very little time diagnosing and addressing prosopagnosia during training at university. This is understandable: up until recently, the condition was thought to be a rare phenomenon, only resulting from known brain trauma, and it was believed that one would be highly unlikely to encounter face recognition deficit in careers that involved working with children. Given this, it is therefore common for professionals to miss the opportunity to diagnose prosopagnosia early. Like dyslexia, which was identified long before educators came to address it, prosopagnosia is increasingly becoming understood but not usually addressed on the educational level.

This information gap needs to be closed, at least in terms of educator awareness of what prosopagnosia is, because identifying one's facial recognition issues may give important insight to the person concerned. Once these are identified, the individual can begin to seek effective strategies toward gaining the identity information that she needs. Although the best and most effective strategies for addressing face recognition deficit have not as yet been identified, it is useful to begin to explore these questions so that each child does not have to invent the wheel alone. If the prosopagnosia is missed because the child "looks fine," and if she is a child for whom prosopagnosia poses a significant obstacle, this can result in missed opportunities for discovering important information that can lead to improved social coping. Let's nip that problem in the bud!

## Making sure how not to identify prosopagnosia

Here are some hints about what to avoid doing when determining whether or not a child has prosopagnosia:

- Do not try to spot a prosopagnosic child simply by looking at a child. To date, prosopagnosics have no specific physical features, observable with the naked eye, that will tell you as to whether or not a child is prosopagnosic. As described in Chapter 1, unlike acquired prosopagnosia, developmental prosopagnosia is not the result of brain trauma. Likewise, remember that prosopagnosia is unrelated to visual acuity. The child may "see" very well—but still have a facial recognition deficit. As previously mentioned, prosopagnosics can usually see and point to the eyes, nose, and mouth. However, faces are processed differently.

- A prosopagnosic child will not usually approach a parent or professional and state, "I cannot recognize faces." These children have lived in their cognitive homes as prosopagnosics all of their lives (unless there is a possibility of later onset developmental prosopagnosia), and they probably view their manner of seeing as normal. It is not helpful to simply ask a child, "Do you recognize faces?"

- When a child recognizes her non-prosopagnosic mother, father, grandmother, or other caregiver at home—or even at school—this does not demonstrate that she has face recognition ability. Common sense tells us that the brunette woman living in the home is mother, the gray-haired woman is grandmother, the black-haired male visitor is uncle, etc. Remember that prosopagnosia is a cogno-visual issue: the individual's intellect is still very much intact!

- Furthermore, there are degrees of prosopagnosia. Children may have learned non-facial methods for recognizing family members—for example, out of predictable context—and had ample time and opportunity for practice. Other senses, or even other aspects of vision, may be used to recognize and identify. A child may recognize the frequently seen professional and a few other people, but this does not mean that there are no problems with facial identification. She may know a particular administrator because there is only one person who enters the classroom at a particular time. She may simply know you as that man or woman who comes and takes her to another room for 30 minutes once a week, or who stands in front of Room 14, or who usually wears her hair up in a bun. If you are male, she may recognize that you have a moustache or tap your foot a lot. She may say, "Good morning, Mrs. Amrock," but she may not be recognizing you by your face.

- Prosopagnosic children may also experience empathy, and it is inappropriate to suggest that expressing significant empathy means that a child can recognize faces well.

Chapter 6

# HOW PROSOPAGNOSICS RECOGNIZE

Let's take a look at looking.

Try looking at a photograph of a face of a man or a woman in a book or magazine and then cover it up. Close your eyes for a moment. What do you remember? Go someplace like a café and look at the people around you. Peek at someone for a minute or more, then close your eyes. Do you still know that person's face? How about if you try to remember someone whom you met for an hour yesterday?

What a prosopagnosic will remember will vary, depending upon the individual. Some remember form, the general shape of the head, hair, style, hair color, complexion. Others may depend upon clothes or race to remember. Were you to draw on a page what you remember, what would you draw?

If one is prosopagnosic, a simple change such as donning a pair of sunglasses, putting on a sweatshirt, or wearing a marching band uniform may render a friend unrecognizable, although there are non-facial clues that will sometimes aid recognition. Imagine talking with a girl inside a building and then not recognizing her one hour later because she has put up her hair up into a ponytail and is wearing sunglasses. For some prosopagnosics, this can lead to confusion.

Understanding the individual perceptive strength of a child can give you insight into strategies to provide relevant information, whether communicating about others or aiming to predict the kinds of changes that may confuse him.

It is important for those who live and work with prosopagnosic children to understand the ways in which those with face recognition deficit sometimes identify others. The following list of commonly used non-facial identity clues is by no means comprehensive, nor does it reflect how every child with prosopagnosia identifies others. Rather, it is offered as a starting point, a suggestion of some of the ways in which prosopagnosics navigate the social world. Other ideas can easily be found by doing a simple internet search for information about prosopagnosia.

## NON-FACIAL IDENTITY CLUES

### Clothing type, color, and style

Clothing can help some prosopagnosics to identify others, but this is often a temporary clue that a child can latch onto. Recognizing coat or hat color or style can be extremely useful, and clothing provides a readily visible clue. However, the child may become confused if, for example, a friend who normally wears a blue coat appears at the supermarket in a red one. A camp counselor whose group will change clothes in the evening needs to be mindful of the possible confusion when people change clothes—for example, to go swimming or when it gets cooler and children change into sweatshirts. It may be necessary to facilitate accordingly in a sensitive and discreet manner.

Potential area of confusion: people sometimes change their clothes throughout the day, and so the clues related to clothing are usually temporary. The prosopagnosic needs to learn that clothing will not always work as an identity source.

### Props (sunglasses, crutches, wheelchair, cigarettes, jewelry, etc.)

For some children with prosopagnosia, these clues are very useful in determining identity. Although some props, such as cigarettes and sunglasses, may be temporary, other clues such as crutches or a particular item of jewelry constantly worn can be quite helpful.

Potential area of confusion: once the props are missing, some prosopagnosics may be without clues as to the fact that they are looking at a familiar person.

### Hair color, style, length, texture, general neatness or messiness, hairline

Interestingly, just as it is normal for infants to recognize by looking at the hairline, as discussed in Chapter 2, prosopagnosics sometimes recognize others by looking at the shape and boundary of the hair, or the hairline. Given this, changes to hairstyle or color may take away this useful identity clue. It may help the prosopagnosic to know in advance if such a change is going to take place.

Potential area of confusion: even putting one's hair up (or letting it down to hang straight) can result in a lack of identity knowledge. While the styles nowadays may result in people frequently changing their hair color, at least people don't usually change their hair color several times a day.

## Facial hair (beard, moustache, specific shape of moustache, eyebrows, etc.)

Facial hair, like that atop the head, sometimes provides relevant clues to prosopagnosics. For example, if most of the men in a room have shaven faces, the prosopagnosic may recognize the one man who has a beard. Conversely, if most men are bearded, it may be easier for the prosopagnosic to recognize the one unbearded man.

Potential area of confusion: while facial hair can provide useful clues, it is less useful when many in the same room have similar facial hair. Therefore, a change of context can be a bit jarring. For example, one may usually recognize "Mike," who is the only bearded person at family reunions. However, if Mike is one of a group of bearded men in a less practiced context, then the ability to recognize him may be limited.

## Face marks (acne, wrinkles, moles, scars, face piercings, etc.)

Face marks such as acne, wrinkles, position and size of moles, scars and face piercings can provide important identity clues for the prosopagnosic. If a person has several lines on her forehead or a nose ring, for example, these can be quite helpful in determining identity.

## Body shape and height (pear-shaped, lanky, tall, petite, slim, heavy set, husky, etc.)

Body shape and height can provide useful clues, although these are qualities that will change as the child and his peers grow.

## Behavior

Scratching one's chin, constantly rubbing a beard, waving an arm about when talking, taking a walk in the morning, sitting on the stoop, whistling, tapping, tilting one's head—these all provide behavioral clues sometimes relevant to a prosopagnosic in determining identity. Other kinds of clues may include conversation topics and habits, such as speaking a lot about sports, taking long strides when walking, or talking hesitantly, braggingly, or talking with one's mouth full.

## Community

The prosopagnosic child may recognize Cindy because she is the tall brunette child who is always with Betsy, whom the child, for some reason, recognizes.

## Voice (pitch, rhythm, tone, accent, lisps, etc.)

The quality of a person's voice can provide a significant recognition hint for some prosopagnosics. Given this, for those who have strength in this area, sometimes starting a conversation will elicit important identity information.

## Facial expressions

These can provide identity information to some prosopagnosics, as will be described in greater detail in Chapter 12.

## Gait (long strides, speed of gait, limp, etc.)

People usually have a particular "profile," a particular gait, and this is something that some prosopagnosics will consciously or subconsciously notice.

## Race (Asian, African American, Latino, Caucasian, etc.)

Some prosopagnosics may not effectively recall skin color or complexion, however.

## Context of place, time, and event

Whether a child usually sees a person behind a desk, in a street directing traffic, at Register 8 at the market, hunched over a garden bed next door, or slumped in front of the town diner, the context can actually provide an identity clue.

## Being drawn to those one recognizes

It is worth considering that, although not always the case, some children may be subconsciously drawn to others who are easiest to identify. This may include, for example, a person with an unusual hairstyle or color or a face marking. If Billy has a mole on his face, for example, Danny may be more willing to initiate an interaction with him. Any of the clues described earlier can contribute to the prosopagnosic's tendency to gravitate toward a particular individual. In addition, as Glenn Alperin has described, the one adult in a classroom of children may be the easiest person for the prosopagnosic child to recognize. The relationship with the recognized adult may become the strongest for the child, because he is drawn to that person, for example.

A child may use any combination of these or other strategies. In addition, a prosopagnosic child will not always be able to accurately and completely answer the question, "Which strategies help you to most effectively recognize people?" and, indeed, it is highly likely that he will believe that his face perception is normal and that he is recognizing by looking at faces, as most sighted people do. Given this, the kinds of observations and errors that the child makes can lend insight into how he discerns identity.

Please be advised that, although some of these characteristics can provide useful identity clues, others are temporary, particularly during adolescence. The child may end a school year saying goodbye to one group of friends and start the next seeing the same peers with changed body heights and shapes, new hair styles, etc.

Various websites offer excellent information on this topic and should be reviewed. Please check the Bibliography as a starting point. Other websites can be found via an internet search for information about prosopagnosia.

## THE FLIP SIDE OF THE UPSIDE-DOWN FACE QUESTION

What does looking at a picture of an upside-down face have to do with face recognition deficit?

It should be noted that prosopagnosics have been found to perform better at matching upside-down face tasks than non-prosopagnosics, and some people argue that this skill reflects facial processing in a manner that is not "holistic,"—that is, it does not involve mentally turning the entire face upside down at once. (Farah *et al.* 1995; Behrman *et al.* 2005; Busigny *et al.* 2008) The ability to recognize an inverted face would be more difficult if that face were perceived "holistically," according to this theory. In other words, turning one face part at a time—an eye or a mouth, for example—would be a much easier mental task than doing the same with an entire face. The theory suggests, therefore, that lack of holistic processing skill for faces enables prosopagnosics to perform these tasks more effectively than non-prosopagnosics. This skill of holistic processing, which normally appears by age four months, may be missing for at least some prosopagnosics. As described earlier in Chapter 2, it appears that, generally speaking, infants process faces in a non-holistic manner prior to about four to five months of age.

## A note about self-recognition:

Given that it is sometimes difficult for prosopagnosics to recognize others when they change, for example, their hair style or hair color, making such changes for a prosopagnosic can also be important, in terms of self-recognition. Some prosopagnosics have stated that they dislike making frequent changes to their hair or other superficial aspects of their appearance, in part because the person in the mirror looks so utterly different to them. One who perceives faces normally would likely find it disconcerting to wake up and see a different face in the mirror, as it is important to have a sense of "self." Since prosopagnosics do not view their faces as identity markers, it appears that those recognizable qualities do become important.

## THE SOCIAL GRACES

It may be useful for those with normal face processing skills to comprehend some of the kinds of errors that those with face recognition deficit sometimes make. Understanding this may make it possible to predict and/or avoid some of those errors, and to attempt to deal with them effectively when they do occur.

Among considerations for the topic of errors are issues of a child's safety as well as self-esteem, as we refer back to Maslow's theory. These two areas need to be addressed for the growing child, and, certainly, frequent errors on tasks that most people commonly perform with ease can be of concern. In some ways, generally helping a child to learn to accept his limitations gracefully—while still celebrating talent—is crucial.

During an interview, Jim, the acquired prosopagnosic quoted at the beginning of this book, described a mistake that any prosopagnosic would dread. He spoke of how he went on a date and sat at a table with the wrong individual, although he quickly explained that he didn't give a rat's "petuchi" about making errors.

He had been at a diner in Queens, New York, and, as he tells it, the diners in Queens are more like restaurants than "diners," with people from all over the world eating there because New York is such "a melting pot." The place was big, 50 to 75 tables, Jim explained, and one could get a BLT or a steak or fish dinner. The menu boasted "like 176 different entrees." And a memorable incident in the world of a prosopagnosic occurred here. Jim stated:

> My date had short, brown hair... We were in a restaurant... I excused myself to use the men's room... And I went back to the table from

the men's room, I wasn't 100 percent positive exactly where our table was, but oop, there's a female sitting by herself, short brown hair… I thought I'd…I went over and sat down at the table with her. Wasn't my date… My date had been waiting for me to wave to give me directions back to the table, like a landlord, and she saw me sit at the wrong table.

Jim continued, reflecting on his own face recognition issues:

Okay, when she [the woman who was a stranger] looked up with a shocked expression on her face, "Why is this strange man sitting at my table?"… My date was already—had already run across the restaurant, and the two of us explained to her that I can't recognize faces and hey, same color hair, same length hair, and I just made a boo boo… I made a mistake, I make mistakes every day I get out of bed… You were walking tall until somebody stepped on your hat!

At some point in a prosopagnosic's life, we realize that we must either sink or swim, have an ability to laugh with life or to be conquered by our errors. It is important for the individual to learn not only how to strive toward navigating social networks, despite the face recognition impairment, but also to cope with identity errors when they do occur, to minimize limitations and find a way in which to be comfortable in one's own skin. This is a crucial challenge. Prosopagnosics tend to have their war stories and, while some are innocent or embarrassing, others are downright risky—for example, they may involve getting into a wrong car or talking with a potentially dangerous person. Whether one is introducing oneself to (or for that matter, ignoring) a friend who has just donned a pair of sunglasses, sitting down with someone with whom one has recently bickered at a party, or navigating a black tie or uniformed event with few clues as to who is who, some prosopagnosics will at least consider having a strategy for identifying potential areas of error, and perhaps developing a sense of humor too. Finding ways in which to encourage risk and successful play with regard to faces, when confronted with such errors, can be a relevant challenge.

The following is a partial list, intended as a springboard for discussion, of some of the common errors that prosopagnosics make, along with descriptions of them. It is possible that some prosopagnosics or researchers may have developed different names for these same errors in describing them.

## Twinning

A prosopagnosic thinks that one person in two or more different contexts is two (or more) different people. For example, a child may see one person in the classroom and that same person in the gym in different clothes, but think that he is looking at two different people in each context. This error can prevent the prosopagnosic child from using knowledge or information about the individual in varied contexts. While this is not always harmful to relationships, it can be. For example, if the prosopagnosic fails to greet the "known" individual in one of the settings, that person may become hurt. Likewise, specific information about the individual (for example, knowing that another child has recently had a leg injury) may prevent the prosopagnosic child from offering help and engaging in other acts of friendship.

> I once made the following mistake: I was working at a particular location and sometimes I saw one woman, a colleague, in one part of the building. I then saw a woman who I thought was a different individual in a different room in the same building. One day, I suddenly realized that they were actually the same person. Unfortunately, my words escaped too soon, and I exclaimed, "I used to think that you were two people, but now I realize you're only one!" The expression on her face really made me wish for a minute that I didn't recognize emotional facial expressions. (Rochelle Ducette, prosopagnosic)

## Merging

A prosopagnosic thinks that two or more people are actually one person. For example, is the receptionist that one sees on Monday at 7:00 am the same person that he sees at 11:00 am, if that receptionist is wearing a uniform, has a similar hairstyle, is of the same race, and is doing the same kind of work? Sometimes these are actually two different people. If a child's friend, Carla, in science class, is very kind and the prosopagnosic child thinks that "Carla," also in art, is not very friendly or ignoring her, this can be confusing to the prosopagnosic child. In fact, the prosopagnosic may be encountering a completely different child in the art class.

## Blending

Blending is the error that occurs when several people appear who have shared identity traits. For example, the prosopagnosic may usually recognize black-haired Linda. However, if he suddenly encounters several females with black hair of the same length, he may find himself not recognizing his friend. Please note that the error of non-recognition, and the opportunity for error, are "enhanced" by several "like" people being in one location.

## Non-recognition

A prosopagnosic does not realize that the person is even vaguely familiar, simply because the usual identity clues (if there ever were any) are gone. This sometimes happens to everybody, including normally face-sighted individuals. However, for some prosopagnosics, it is a constant problem.

## Mistaken identity

A prosopagnosic thinks that he knows who the individual is—but he is wrong. Again, this error can also occur with anybody normally sighted.[1] It is the fact that this kind of error may be typical of prosopagnosics' identity interactions that make it an important issue here.

> There's certain people that I liked, and I recognized the girls in my row. One girl in my row because she had a broken arm, and she always went to school with one arm that did not work at all [and who wore a cast], but she was very smart. And whenever I asked her for help, she would always help me with the work. Now I didn't have to say too much. She was the type that didn't talk too much, but she was very, very nice, so I sort of liked her. (Donna, developmental prosopagnosic)

Donna uses non-facial clues to recognize people and, like other prosopagnosics, she has come to depend upon the visual hints for identifying others that may be more time-consuming than face recognition is for most. Which kinds of clues are useful to the individual will depend upon memory strength in various areas. While some may focus upon clothing color and style, for example, those who understand facial expressions may notice particular constellations of emotion typically expressed by the individual. Still other prosopagnosics may find that gesture—or any combination of these—or even some other characteristics provide relevant identity clues.

---

1   Although there are other cognitive impairments unrelated to visual acuity that some children may have, please note that in this book the term "normally sighted" is used to mean "non-prosopagnosic."

## Chapter 7

# SUPPORTING THE CHILD IN ELEMENTARY SCHOOL

Note to parents: if you would like your child's teacher to learn about prosopagnosia, but her reading time is very limited, you might consider bookmarking the following sections specifically on the topic of teaching strategy.

The unrecognized world of faces can offer tricky terrain for the developing child, and having strategies for successfully negotiating its many twists and turns may contribute to her success in the social realm.

Ideas offered here are intended to help the prosopagnosic child to cope with non-recognition, so that she is included in school and community activities. Please remember that she should continue to be intellectually stretched in many areas.

This list is intended to offer a springboard, and it is important to keep in mind the words of one parent of a deaf child who described to me her own experience of supporting her child and the need to follow her own intuition, even if it countered the current trends. At the time that her daughter had been given a cochlear implant, the medical protocol was different from what it is now. That parent actually defied some of the known protocol of the day and provided her child with the chance to use the cochlear implant in one ear and a hearing aid in the other, because the mother had reasoned that one ear could teach the other to hear, as the child moved from a familiar to an unfamiliar world of sound. (At the time, it had been suggested by the child's audiologist that hearing aids remain turned off.) Today, however, the protocol has changed to reflect what this mother had determined to do on her own. Likewise, parents should rely on their own instincts about their child and refrain from embarking on activities or strategies that simply do not appear supportive to their individual child's needs.

There are several considerations for teachers and administrators who wish to contribute to the prosopagnosic child's gaining the identity information to which others regularly have easy access, and which commonly contributes to developing social understanding. As the goal of inclusion requires that the teacher create classroom activities and free-time structures effective for everyone, it may be necessary to rethink some everyday activities. Once the teacher "gets the hang of it," it should become easy and second nature to offer fun activities that may mean the world of difference to the prosopagnosic, while also providing worthwhile learning activities to all of the children in the class.

## NAME LABELS

Name labels, perhaps more appropriate in elementary school, are tricky because, as is the case with any activity or classroom "business" issue, they need to be relevant to all students—not just the prosopagnosic child. If the child with face recognition deficit knows how to read, however, they can obviously be truly helpful in offering identity information.

Consider finding a strategy for getting people in elementary grades to wear name labels, if at all possible. For example, children can make and wear name tags or name necklaces for the first day or first week of classes. If incorporated into an art activity, each student can create name tags that enable each child to express herself, thereby providing consistent written clues that are artistic and colorful for the prosopagnosic child, while offering a fun activity for everyone.

A variation to extend this activity may work for some classes. A particularly creative teacher (who doesn't mind the extra prep time) may be able to motivate children to wear name labels daily by, for example, writing a yellow sticky message for each student on the back of the name label each day. For instance, if the students leave their name labels in a classroom basket or box at the end of each day, the teacher can quickly go through the basket and write a message that will greet each child in the morning. The teacher may write, "Sammy, I liked your work in math yesterday" and tape that yellow sticky to the back of Sammy's name label, while providing individualized labels for other children too. The students may then treasure their hidden messages while wearing their name tags daily. They can remove the messages, or stick them on any papers that they bring home that day.

Another way of providing clear identity information for students would be to have them make name signs for the sides of their desks as a first week of class art activity. They can keep those signs up during the year and design new ones throughout the year, one for each season. A little paper, crayons, markers, and tape can go a long way in addressing identity issues and making life easier for the prosopagnosic child.

Note: teachers should realize that outside of the classroom—for example, in the schoolyard—or without children sitting in their seats, the prosopagnosic child may lack access to "who's who" information. Nonetheless, such signs can be extremely useful.

## CLASSROOM STRATEGIES

Certain classroom strategies, if carefully and tactfully applied, may effectively include the prosopagnosic child. These methods involve providing hints in a manner that is discreet, and also offering class and activity structures that take into account the face recognition deficit. For example, just as a teacher would be careful not to ask a child who is colorblind to go to the front of the class and point to the red and green circles on a traffic light display, so, too, should the teacher be thoughtful in working with the prosopagnosic child.

Given that there may be a prosopagnosic child in your group, reconsider first-day name games. Organize, instead, fun activities on the first day which will build a warm, fun class climate and enable students to get to know one another—without their having to memorize faces. Let every child shine.

Within the class, frequently use other children's names. Even though David recognized "Billy" yesterday, he may not recognize him today—if Billy is wearing a hat or different clothes or sitting in a different seat. For example, when calling on students, don't point to them and say, "Yes, what do you think?" Instead, ask, "Susan, what do you think?" Likewise, refrain from selecting a prosopagnosic child to pass back papers by looking at names and handing them back to each person. It would be acceptable, however, to ask the prosopagnosic to pass out blank papers, one to each child, for class activities, when needed.

When offering instructions that involve the children working with others, make sure to give the prosopagnosic child something to do that is a reachable goal. Provide clues. "Steve (who is non-prosopagnosic), go join Josh (the prosopagnosic child)." Let the child feel confident and happy. You should *not* simply say, "Okay, everybody, join your partners. Josh (who is prosopagnosic), your partner is Steve (non-prosopagnosic)." Bewilderment is not a healthy way in which to begin a task. Children need activities to start off well, to create the best springboard for confidence and success.

Alternatively, you may point to each child as you group them and also use their names, but make sure that the prosopagnosic child is paying attention when you point, if you do so. Be aware that some have difficulty with following gaze, a skill that normally sighted children will develop by about 12 months. A tip that Glenn Alperin suggests is that sometimes pointing, combined with mentioning a non-facial feature, may be helpful for a prosopagnosic to understand exactly who is being identified (for example [while pointing], "Sammy, why don't you join our friend, Peter, who looks so nice in his blue and white striped shirt today.")

Be sensitive about groupings and class structures, particularly if the children move from one classroom to the next throughout the day. A child may work well with students in one class but not recognize some of them in the next one.

Racially diverse groupings might be helpful for some prosopagnosic children and also fantastic for helping to build a wonderfully harmonious experience for everyone. Groupings that involve the child's working with those who all have different hair color and/or hairstyles are also useful.

If there are circle activities in the class, you might discreetly and sensitively make sure that someone whom the prosopagnosic student recognizes is sitting nearby. Simply tell students to have a seat and, as students are sitting, you might say, for example, "Larry, why don't you sit here? Great!" You can also vary this by intentionally naming the person who has sat beside the prosopagnosic: "Okay, Stacey (the child sitting next to the prosopagnosic), good, you've found a spot." Again, make sure that the prosopagnosic sees that you are talking to the person sitting next to her. Be sensitive. Make sure not to single the prosopagnosic child out.

Use strategies other than simple name strategies for identification. For example, instead of simply telling children, "If you need paint, Marcy will help you" if all children are mingling and Marcy is one of them, make sure to clearly identify Marcy. Rather, give Marcy a kind of big or honorary ribbon to wear that will help her to feel proud and will provide identification for the prosopagnosic child, as well as others.

The question of disclosure of prosopagnosia is an important one that may follow the child for many years to come, and it will be discussed more extensively in Chapter 10. Do not "out" a prosopagnosic child on your own. Talk with the parent and child about this issue. This is important not only for ethical reasons and those related to the effectiveness of teaching, but also in terms of legal issues related to confidentiality. If parent and child do want to be open about the prosopagnosia, discuss the issue with the family ahead of time and be thoughtful about whether and how you introduce this to the class. Attitude and tone are everything in teaching. Setting a climate of acceptance and respect is key.

If the child is "open" about the prosopagnosia, you might want to informally assign another child in the class to act as an occasional buddy, but only if this can be done in a manner that doesn't make the child feel too dependent on others (or "like a baby"); building the child's self-esteem is crucial. For the child who is open about the face recognition deficit, consider, with the permission of her parent or caregiver, the possibility of sensitively educating the other children about prosopagnosia, so that they can learn to be a friend to the child. Given that little was known about prosopagnosia in the past, such an act should probably be considered experimental in nature, and it would need to be offered with sensitivity and wisdom. While this could make life much easier for everyone, as other children understand that they may need to say hello first and hint at or indicate their names, it also has the potential to make the prosopagnosic child feel awkward. This needs to be done carefully, with full awareness that if openness occurs in an environment less than nurturing of diversity, bullying may become a problem.

Such teaching tools as a children's coloring book in which clothes and hairstyle are a focus, for example, could also help.

If the prosopagnosic child is in a school where uniforms are worn by students and/or teachers, you might want to talk with the parent about whether this is truly the best environment for her (Alperin 2002). I believe that I speak for many prosopagnosics when I say that being in a school in which students wear uniforms is a situation that the child should not have to confront.

Realize that any activities that require a jumbling of children—for example, jumping around activities, in which children are in no particular order—may be confusing in terms of face or name recognition for the prosopagnosic child. Such games are sometimes unavoidable, but consider strategies for keeping the child included (that is, calling other children by name, etc., or following up the game with something more settled, in which recognition may be a bit easier).

Use your own common sense in giving the child with face recognition deficit roles in school activities. Don't exclude her: provide as many learning opportunities as possible to enable her to stretch socially, but act intentionally to offer activities at which she will succeed.

Rather than wasting a lot of her time with too much experimenting, find out how the child *does* recognize people and help her learn to exploit her abilities in this area, to get better at using the visual skills that she has. For example, if the child is good at recognizing clothes, you might suggest that she does an informal scan of children at their desks and what they are wearing in the morning. Remember, however, that if the other children change their clothes in any way, for example, if Mary puts on a hat before going outside or Pat takes off his sweater—these clues can be rendered useless, depending upon the prosopagnosic. In addition, do not spend too much time at this, and do not think that you can "teach" the child to recognize faces using this strategy. I know one person who did this as a child, and he says that it did not help him very much.

Realize that many prosopagnosics do not find much benefit in using photos to help recognize people. If you want to try this or have an idea that you think will help a child to cope, then realize that sometimes it is possible to hit upon something that will work. However, be respectful of the child's time. If you have seen face recognition programs that have already been tested and are proven to work, by all means try them, but in a limited way. Childhood is a neurologically fertile time of life—there is great potential for learning and it is not uncommon for prosopagnosics to be highly academically talented. A good teacher is able to switch gears when an activity is ineffective, and to keep the priorities on offering the child relevant life skills and knowledge. If you are normally sighted, faces might be extremely important for you. However, other things are important to the prosopagnosic. Faces aren't everything. You, as a teacher, need to accept diversity. Let the child spend an appropriate amount of time developing talent areas.

Paying more attention to faces does not usually help the prosopagnosic. As is the case with dyslexics, who for many years were sometimes considered to be "lazy" about reading until the cognovisual issue was recognized, so, too, do prosopagnosics lack face recognition ability that is unrelated to motivation. Do not keep trying to force prosopagnosic children to pay attention to faces, in an attempt to help them to recognize people more effectively.

For the child who doesn't read facial expressions well, it may be a good idea to get her a manners book suitable for children, so that she can become socially conscious and aware of manners and social expectations. These may need to be taught explicitly and should be age appropriate (see Chapter 12, for ideas about this). It may be useful also to provide ways in which other children can explicitly and politely offer information that is usually offered non-verbally. For example, classmates may be learning at home to exercise restraint, and *not* to say, "That gets me mad, stop it" or "Gross—you're talking with your mouth full!" Given that the prosopagnosic child may lack ability to read emotional expressions, it may be helpful for other children to be taught to politely express themselves in a manner that is more direct but still caring, when interacting with the prosopagnosic child. The tactful guidance of an adult may be needed to help children.

Include the child. In other words, address the prosopagnosic's needs discreetly and sensitively, always keeping in mind the "whole child," as you would do for any student needing help in a particular area. Don't constantly point out difference. This may be obvious but, as an example, there is a difference between "Billy (non-prosopagnosic), could you join Sammy (prosopagnosic) to clean up the paint?" and "Sammy, this boy over here is Billy" (implied: who has been in the same classroom with you for three months). "He'll help you with the paints." The former is a discreet question that gives Sammy necessary information (who Billy is) and is far more tactful than the latter. Remember also that some prosopagnosics may begin to recognize some or all of the students in a class at some point. Leave room for this to occur. Don't let the student flounder but, likewise, let her use the relevant and effective skills that the prosopagnosic child has.

Logistical information—since getting information often requires recognizing a particular person in order to elicit it, lack of face recognition skills may result in logistical difficulties, such as not giving lunch money to the correct individual (unless that person is in the same place every day). Keep in touch. Help when possible, but also celebrate the child's own clever ways of managing the situation. Try not to let prosopagnosia be at the forefront, but rather, let an understanding of prosopagnosia lead to ideas for navigating the social world, whether by keeping a secret, seeking and finding a friend, etc., so that the child can focus on developing talents in other areas.

If you meet and work with one prosopagnosic, do not assume when you meet another that the experience will be the same. Remember that not all prosopagnosics are alike. There is significant diversity among prosopagnosic—and all—children. The extent of the prosopagnosia itself, the severity of the face recognition deficit, and even the question as to whether it is an obstacle will vary depending upon the individual.


## RECESS AND PLAYTIME AT SCHOOL

I used to go on a swing and they had like a roof on top of the swing that went all the way down. So when I was on the swing, I used to try to touch the top of the roof. In other words, I made up my own thing, not just swinging, but trying to touch the top of the roof. Then they had a sandbox, so I liked making things in the sandbox, like little houses. I used to make a little village. I liked making little villages, like roads that I'd make, like a round circle, then I'd make like a fence around it made out of sand. So they let us have water, if we wanted to, so in order to keep the houses together that we were building, I'd put a little water on it... You had to have something that will stick it, that would stick it together. I never had any kids near me. I didn't have any friends there. I did it by myself. (Donna, developmental prosopagnosic)

I remember one situation in particular...must have been outside of the playground or something or other... somebody was either teasing me or hitting me...and I went over and I can't remember if I slugged him or if I bit him... And afterwards, the teacher came up to me and asked me why I did that and I said, "Because 'he' did this to me"... and the teacher said [to the other child], "Did you do this to him?" The kid said, "No, I didn't do this to him." I didn't know at the time. I wasn't sure if I had gotten the right one. I can't excuse my behavior because... My behavior still would have been poor in the first place... but that was certainly my first memory of having this specific problem of recognizing faces. I didn't know one way or the other... And I don't think that educationally, I learned probably as much as I could have in those four years. But there really wasn't a better place for me back then. (Glenn, childhood-acquired prosopagnosia)

Unstructured free-time activities may provide welcome solitude for any child who needs this, but they can also be among the most challenging for those prosopagnosic children who wish to spend time socializing with others. Whereas one can sometimes determine who is who by looking at familiar groupings of desks in the classroom, it can be very difficult to find known people in the amorphous gatherings of children in the schoolyard, lunchroom, or other school assembly areas.

There are ways in which to provide support to those prosopagnosic children who find themselves involuntarily alone during recess time. Consider suggesting a game to a group of children during recess and include the prosopagnosic child in that game. Offer daily structured activities for those who choose to participate in them. Consider a buddy system for anyone who wishes to have a recess friend, not only including prosopagnosics, but available to any child who wishes to participate. And remember that some children do want and need unstructured time—and even a chance to be alone a bit. Make sure, however, that there are options for the prosopagnosic child who wants to have a playmate and literally cannot find one. Some prosopagnosics may be understandably reluctant to take the initiative in social interactions, and they may instead wait for others to approach them. Offering structures that provide playmates for those who wish to find one can be helpful.

A final note on schoolyard games: when organizing them for younger children—for example, in grades one to three—consider sometimes slightly revising games that rely on names and faces. For example, if playing Red Rover, a game that requires a child to call on another child to run to her group, the teacher may revise the game so that, instead of the child's saying, "Send Jason right over," it is played as, "Send pink shirt, black pants right over." This can add a playful variation to the game, while creating a fair playing field for the prosopagnosic child.

## CAFETERIA

> Remember those chairs I told you about, in the lunchroom, that looked like a seesaw. Well, the chairs had one big iron bar under the table and a round stool on each side of the table. Now let's say a person was heavy, my side of the stool would go up. And when I sat down, her side of the stool went up. So it was like a little seesaw. So I used to like it. And the same girl always used to run to her side of the stool, because she liked it when she played that game with the stools... (Donna, developmental prosopagnosic)

A child may unknowingly lack the option to initiate social interactions and need to wait to be approached. "That's my friend, who usually plays with me at lunch time, I think that I'll go sit with her and her other friends" may not be an option when that child is indistinguishable from others. Depending upon the set-up of your cafeteria, make sure that the prosopagnosic has a group of friends with whom to sit. Consider lunch buddies, topic tables (for example, children who like comic books might have a particular table at which they may choose to sit). Put a sign on the table with a picture of a comic book and the words, "comic book table." Also think about simple but well-planned and effective nudging to assure that the child has a lunch time friend.

## SAFETY

Some prosopagnosics have noted a problem with bullying in school and in their neighbhoods. Prevent bullying and keep your eyes open for it, so that you can stop it the moment you notice its signs. The prosopagnosic child has two major problems with regard to bullying and violence in general. First, there is the difficulty with identifying the assailant when reporting a threat or an attack. Second, there is the challenge of not being able to later avoid the "known" assailant, because of the facial recognition issues. Talk with the child before she ever faces the issue of bullying. Remember that she may not realize who is doing the bullying, and this could create a truly unsafe situation. Discreetly keep your eye out, but be proactive too. Do not waste the child's precious years in an unsafe environment. Indeed, removing her from a school in which bullying is a constant threat may be a significant step taken in her education. As Maslow (1943) has noted (see Chapter 4), safety is a fundamental need, and important for a child's development in more sophisticated ways. Glenn Alperin described bullying that he experienced for years, an issue made more severe by the fact that he could not identify his attackers:

> ...bullying and that kind of stuff...really overshadowed a lot of my value of myself, a lot of my interpretation of social situations...made me want I think to become more mature as a coping mechanism, rather than being more sociable and putting myself out there and risking social rejection...made me want to become more withdrawn. (Glenn, childhood-acquired prosopagnosia)

Bullying may also have an impact on a child's self-esteem. Remember, if her face recognition skills are so severely impaired that she does not know who has done the bullying, then this becomes not an issue of "someone's" picking on her, but rather of "everyone's" picking on her. Certainly, this can have a serious impact on her sense of physical and emotional security and, if unaddressed, her self-esteem.

All too often, adults accept bullying as an inevitable rite of childhood. This has got to stop. Few adults would accept getting regularly beaten up by their neighbors. Why should we allow our children enduring pain, ridicule, and general cruelty that we, ourselves, would not endure? Children must be fully protected: bullying should never be tolerated.

## ACTIVITIES

As discussed in Chapter 4, there appears to be a correlation between atypical processing of motion and prosopagnosia. A child's reaction to faces is important and may, indeed, even influence the kinds of activities to which she is drawn. For example, one who finds faces to be repelling (if, for example, as Grandin (2006) suggests, facial motion is bothersome to her) may prefer a quiet beach to a loud, crowded carnival. A prosopagnosic who is good at recognizing facial expressions may feel comfortable in groups and enjoy socializing, because much of the communicated social content will be grasped. One of the great challenges for a caregiver or professional is in determining how much social activity is necessary for a child to learn to get along well with others in social groups, a necessary life skill. Sean Barron and Temple Grandin's book (2005), *The Unwritten Rules of Social Relationships: Decoding Social Mysteries Through the Unique Perspectives of Autism*, contains some ideas along these lines.

## BROADER CHOICES (UNIFORMS, ETC.)

Choosing appropriate school environments and activities for a child with face recognition deficit is crucial. As described earlier, the prosopagnosic would do well, if possible, to avoid schools where uniforms are always required. Keep in mind as a parent, however, that there may be times when your child's love for the activity, need for inclusion with peers, or goals with regard to the activity itself, will surpass her potential discomfort in terms of the recognition challenges when all are dressed alike. For example, if your son has a great love of the outdoors and the Boy Scouts provide the best way to learn hiking skills, he may wish to join—despite the uniforms. It is possible that the kinds of activity structures of the organization may render the uniform issues less important. Likewise, if your daughter loves playing the violin and band members need to wear uniforms, this requirement may be less important to her overall growth than the opportunity to learn the discipline of practicing an instrument and performing with others. Teach your child to learn how to make these choices with confidence and to gain skills in many talent areas, while nurturing friendships when possible.

As a teacher, live, celebrate, and learn with your prosopagnosic student—as you would with all of the children in your class!

## Chapter 8

# THE OLDER CHILD AND TEEN IN SCHOOL

Some of the ideas offered in Chapter 7 are also relevant to the teenager and can be slightly adapted for the older child and teen. Those working with this population should examine the ideas discussed there to determine whether any are adaptable and can be made age appropriate, given the particular school climate and developmental stage of the individual prosopagnosic child and the other students. However, this chapter offers some additional ideas for supporting the student in junior high and high school.

In Western cultures, and perhaps in others, there are often issues related to sense of belonging to a peer group that may result in embarrassment for the teen who lacks the ability to recognize faces. As is the case with some visually impaired teenagers, who resist using adaptive technology in a mainstream classroom due to awkwardness stemming from wishing to fit in with a peer group, the prosopagnosic teen may also wish to be like "everyone else." In the less structured environments of the upper grades, where the challenges for the prosopagnosic learner increase, the teacher will need to be sensitive not only to older children's and teens' practical need for identity information, but also to their developmental needs for acceptance by peers and general belonging.

## ADMINISTRATIVE DECISIONS

Consider class size and structure when assigning a prosopagnosic student to classes. For example, if a particular teacher tends to have classes in which there is a lot of physical movement and changing of seats within the class, think about whether this will work for the particular prosopagnosic student and determine whether there is a class whose structure (and teaching style) would be better suited to him. Sometimes there may be trade-offs. For example, perhaps a particular subject is being taught that would truly engage the learner and enable him to stretch his talents. In addition, there are many prosopagnosics who greatly enjoy classes that have many social activities in them. Regardless of whether the class would be "prosopagnosic-friendly," there may be great reasons for his taking it.

Realize that if the student attends a typical public school, there will be many situations throughout a given day in which he will encounter non-recognition issues. For example, when passing other students in the corridor, the prosopagnosic teen will not recognize some of them, and there may at times be a risk of social repercussions for non-recognition if these students feel snubbed, however unintentional the "snubbing" may be.

Areas in which students congregate in an unstructured, unpredictable manner will likely provide challenges for the prosopagnosic student. If appropriate and the student is open about non-recognition, given the school climate, a buddy system might be tried (see the section on buddy systems for older children and teens, Chapter 11.)

Depending upon the student's personality, priorities, and social skills, and the general school climate (including the issue of safety), you might want to consider teaching prosopagnosic teens to be a little outgoing in greeting others (e.g. by nodding the head or giving a little smile and nod when passing others) so that other students—particularly those whom they "know"—do not feel ignored when the prosopagnosic student goes past them. This should only be done if the child can do it skillfully, because it would be counterproductive to have a student who doesn't "get" how to smile slightly offer a broad smile to everyone in the corridors.

As is the case with other students, it may be useful to encourage the learner to join a club at the school that will enable him to share and nurture talents with others who are like-minded. There is nothing like a common hobby or interest to help build friendships.

In some lunchrooms, where there is less structure and more movement among social groups, there may also be many incidences of non-recognition. Given this, whether or not the student is open about the prosopagnosia, keep on the lookout as to whether he is successfully finding people with whom to sit. Act quickly if need be to informally arrange for the child to sit with particular friends during lunch time. Make sure to do so in a manner that is sensitive and discreet. As previously described in the section on elementary school children, the school may even consider some optional lunch tables organized by interest. For example, there could be a few conversation or lunch club tables on the topic of "computers," with the word, "computers" or "music" posted on folded signs on the table.

Realize that illustrations that include many subtleties—raised eyebrows, grimaces, smirks, uplift of the lips, ill-timed, for example—may be less accessible to the prosopagnosic who has difficulty recognizing emotional expression. (Again, as already discussed, some prosopagnosics can see facial expressions quite well—and may even be skilled above the norm at this.)

Some teens, particularly those with Asperger syndrome who do not recognize some emotional facial (or vocal) expressions may find the previously referenced book, *The Unwritten Rules of Social Relationships: Decoding Social Mysteries Through the Unique Perspectives of Autism* (Barron and Grandin 2005), helpful to read, if they are mature enough to do so. There are certain commonly known but unwritten rules that children, teens, and adults should understand regarding what others consider to be acceptable. The book contains some excellent lists regarding manners that might be offered to a teen who would benefit from understanding the kind of information that needs to be made explicit to some children. Also note that there are other books and videos regarding manners (including those available for free on YouTube) that can be found with an online search. These can be valuable for some children, as they can explicitly offer opportunity to learn manners through story or clear instruction. Given that some children will lack visual access to the common social clues, it is only fair that he be offered the tools for succeeding in society. Such factors as the age, interests, personality, and general maturity level of the child —— as well as the parent's own comfort with teaching manners should contribute to determining as to how the child will learn about the important topic of having manners.

## CAREER CHOICES

As already mentioned, prosopagnosics may become professionals in many walks of life. The goal is to guide an individual toward contributing his gifts in a career that will be personally satisfying. When providing guidance to an older child, try to be imaginative and smart in finding ways in which he can do what he loves and is good at. Help the teen to adapt either his coping strategies and/or his career goals for success. If he is interested in politics, for example, see what kinds of jobs there are that would enable success, even without face recognition ability. For example, speech writers and policy analysts can make significant political contributions without requiring as much facial understanding as does an elected politician. Or perhaps the politician can learn great "people" skills without knowing faces, and still become an effective elected representative. If a child lacks access to the broad range of emotional expressions, a job that would require immediate ability to gauge others' emotions may pose a significant challenge, but he may find a related niche in which effectiveness is more readily within reach.

Realistically, prosopagnosia can sometimes influence aspects of career success for many kinds of jobs. Determining who ordered the soup can be a challenge in a restaurant in which patrons tend to mill about—and this may ultimately influence tips if a waiter makes too many identity errors. The difficulty some prosopagnosics have in recognizing some of the main emotional facial expressions can also influence job performance. For example, those working in sales, law, and teaching might depend a great deal upon their ability to gauge others' emotions. Comprehending the difference between an expression of interest versus one that indicates the onset of boredom may be crucial, for example, because it can result in the professional's changing a topic or tactic if necessary. Likewise, catching a facial inconsistency can enable one to distinguish between honesty and dishonesty, an important skill. A lawyer's ability to point to an individual in a courtroom and to ask with certainty, "Is this the man right here that you say committed the crime?" may be limited if there are two average-build, bald men sitting side by side on the bench and hints have not been provided to that prosopagnosic attorney. On the other hand, the many talents that an individual can bring to a job may be worth the facial recognition challenges that he will experience. There are certain logistical issues that can be addressed with thoughtful planning to adapt a job, which may at first appear to be extremely challenging, into a manageable kind of career, in terms of face recognition ability. Logically, for obvious reasons, I do not recommend that prosopagnosics take on jobs in which facial identity information is crucial, such as that of police officer. However, perhaps in the future, technology will enable even that type of career to become attainable for a prosopagnosic.

Developmental prosopagnosics are sometimes highly successful working as mathematicians, sales people, secretaries, lawyers, teachers, engineers, cashiers, full-time moms or dads, or as many other kinds of professionals. As is the case with everyone, developing talents fully and finding a niche is crucial.

## EXPLORING CAREER OPTIONS
### Trial and error

While developmental prosopagnosia will not necessarily influence one's original choice of profession, particularly if the person is unaware of his face recognition deficit and/or consequent limitations, there is likely to be some job-related trial and error related to the cognovisual issue. In some cases, the prosopagnosia may influence whether or not the person stays in a particular kind of position, unless he determines strategies for adapting it to suit his personal skill and talent areas.

For example, a prosopagnosic teacher may prefer to work with adults, who do not jump around quite as much and tend to be comfortable in sitting in predictable groupings, rather than children, for whom identity is not only a social but also a safety issue. Consider, for example, that in some neighborhoods, the teacher must escort a child to the exit at the end of the day to assure that he is picked up by a parent. Not being able to correctly identify the parent could present a serious safety issue. Such a prosopagnosic might need to develop a very effective strategy. Otherwise, he may choose to work with adults, or to find a teaching job with children that minimizes such risks.

Regarding comprehending emotional expression, some people whose ability to perceive expressions is limited may find jobs that do not require one to immediately respond to facial expressions. To extend the teaching example further, while those prosopagnosic educators who recognize facial expressions may be able to thrive in the classroom, the instructor who fails to see many of the broad range of emotional expressions may find it challenging to "pick up" on student needs in the classroom. He may confuse expressions of boredom for those of interest and extend or elaborate upon topics long after the students have drifted off. Such a teacher may be surprised to learn, for example, that those students who had appeared to be engaged were actually quite frustrated. It may be worth considering, in such instances, strategies for compensating for the deficit, whether by reducing learner populations (that is, smaller classes), constant "dipsticking" (creating frequent tools for student feedback), or other strategies. Indeed, even becoming involved in online learning might be useful to those weary from the face recognition issues.

Find ways in which an older child can develop strategies to pursue his talents and passions in a manner that will contribute.

## USING TECHNOLOGY

In terms of the prosopagnosia, as technology becomes more developed and children's options for assistive technology expand, the ability to be inventive, to be flexible, to adapt, and to take the initiative in using technology will be an important skill for the future. Teach a child not only to use the technology currently available to adapt his skills to succeed with prosopagnosia—in school and community and in the years that follow—but also to be his own teacher, to be proactive in seeking ways in which to adapt technology to meet his needs in general. Children need to learn how they can learn most effectively so that they can later teach themselves.

## SUMMARY OF TEACHING TIPS

The parent or professional who is aware of a child's prosopagnosia will need to sensitively and wisely determine how his needs can best be served and talents enhanced, and whether intervention—formal or informal—is needed at all. The neurologically rich potential that childhood offers requires us to use the child's time well, and if the child is already well adapted, an intervention may disrupt and hinder rather than support. Even if the child is having social issues, talent needs to be tapped and time spent bolstering potential.

It is useful to keep in mind that this is *not* to suggest that all prosopagnosics can or should become "social butterflies." We need to accept, embrace, and work with who we are, as we are, although it is important to get along with others socially. Whether the individual is quiet, more comfortable with solitude and small groups than crowds, or is someone who greatly enjoys the buzz of social interaction, this book offers suggestions in the hope that life can be made happier if the lack of face recognition skills is addressed with kindness, compassion, and competence. It is important that solitude—aloneness—be chosen, and not the result of misunderstandings or underdeveloped social skills caused by long-term lack of identity information. Helping a child learn to comprehend the social realm and to minimize such misunderstandings is crucial. Finding ways to include individuals in activities can contribute to their building lifelong social skills, and can have an impact on family life, friendships, community involvement, and professional success.

Chapter 9

# WORKING WITH PARENTS
# AND TEACHERS

While the point cannot be made too strongly that children who are thriving well should be left to flourish without intervention, some parents whose children are severely socially isolated as a result of face recognition deficit may wish to work with teachers or other childcare professionals to address the issue of prosopagnosia. If so, advocate sensitively and assertively to collaborate toward getting your child's needs met. Stay in touch with the school. Find out how your child is doing with regard to the other children, and whether the others are being encouraged to act kindly toward her.

Many teachers like to collaborate with parents, but it may be a challenge to get the prosopagnosia acknowledged. If appropriate, consider talking with the teachers about whether and how your child is being included in the classroom. Remember, teachers may lack adequate time to search out effective resources, even if they care deeply about effectively addressing your child's needs. Those educators may have several classes per day with 20 students or more per class, and which require preparation of activities for all of the students as well as additional administrative paperwork. Be a member of a team working on your child's behalf. Because the teachers are particularly pressed for time, you may consider sensitively and tactfully offering to bring them material about prosopagnosia. Specifically bookmarking the pages related to your child's needs in school may also be helpful. This is a bit delicate, because there is sometimes a fine line between providing invaluable information and telling people how to do their job. Be discreet.

It should go without saying that contact with teachers should also include strategies related to your child's talent areas. Finding tools that will allow your child to explore and to develop abilities in talent areas will provide her with an important gift and nurture a lifelong love of learning. If a teacher does not seem to be tapping your child's areas of talent, that educator may need help and encouragement in determining what these areas are.

Communicate with your child's teachers or other professionals, if relevant, to get information that will help you to reinforce what your child is learning so that you can extend that learning. Likewise, it would be useful to ensure that the right hand knows what the left hand is doing, that professionals working with your child are communicating when that would be of benefit to your child. What is learned at school, in terms of her developing social skills, should be useful to her life outside of school, and practicing such skills in authentic situations is important, although there needs to be a difference between the world of school and the comfort of home. Balancing this will be important. Professionals may communicate about strategies being practiced so that, when relevant, they can be applied to related situations as they occur.

Although it is currently unlikely that one will find a local parental group related to supporting the prosopagnosic child in school, there are online forums that one can use—and opportunities to create others—in order to meet virtually with other people who share the challenge of supporting such a child. And although not all prosopagnosic children are on the autistic spectrum, for those who are, local or online support groups related to these issues may provide valuable resources for parents in search of ideas. Make sure not to use your child's real name online and be protective of her privacy and safety. And remember that at some point in the future she may become a member of that same group and see what you've written, or someone in your community may join the group. Be thoughtful about whether or not to use your own real name in relation to your child's need for privacy.

It is worth considering whether it would be beneficial to your child to have the opportunity to meet other prosopagnosics her age. Sometimes friendships with those sharing a similar perceptive style can be a wonderful way in which to thrive.

Chapter 10

# HELPING THE CHILD TO THRIVE SOCIALLY

## AT HOME AND COMMUNITY

In addressing what will help the prosopagnosic child to maximize his opportunity to thrive, whether at school, at home, or in the community, it is useful to again consider Maslow's hierarchy of needs. A parent and/or other individuals significant in the child's community can contribute to a child's sense of safety, thereby meeting some of the lower level needs, and also address his need for belonging, self-esteem, and opportunity to strive toward self-actualization.

Some prosopagnosic children can use non-facial strategies to identify their parents while others can't. If needed, provide ideas that will enable your child to identify you and others, to learn to navigate the social world, and to address recognition limitations gracefully.

It would be useful to find out how your child *does* recognize people. Focus on helping to find the clues he needs when trying to identify you. For example, if clothing provides strong identity clues, say, "I'll be wearing my purple coat when we meet later today," or "You'll be able to find me in the audience during the recital because I'll be wearing my favorite red top and you'll see my long, black hair in a bun." If your child recognizes voices, offer a friendly hello when he is within earshot. If your hairstyle significantly helps him to identify you, provide fair warning when you are going to get it cut or wear it differently, prior to meeting. Indeed, it may be useful to discuss the haircut days in advance. Also, but only if your child has a severe impairment, consider offering a special, confidential code for recognizing you, whether it be a special hand gesture, whistle as Glenn Alperin recommended during an interview, or password. It will also help his sense of security for you to be where you say you are going to be, when you promise to be there. Context of place and time can be important to prosopagnosics. If you are a person who is chronically late or who tends not to keep commitments regarding time and place, you may have some changing to do in order to get your child's needs met.

While offering your child encouragement to form meaningful friendships and trust, also teach self-protection. As previously mentioned, encourage him to develop skills to protect himself against bullying and other physical threats in the neighborhood, *before* they have a chance to occur. Do not allow him to stay in situations in which there are constant threats to his physical safety; these also present threats to learning, because a healthy sense of safety can free up a child to move on to higher developmental stages, and enable learning to occur.

Beyond the structure of a school environment, the prosopagnosic may face situations that involve forming friendships with those who live in the neighborhood and in the general community. Work to instill a strong sense of self-esteem; encourage your child to be brave and sometimes take the initiative, if physically safe to do so in the particular neighborhood or situation; and encourage an ability to thrive on strength and to acknowledge shortcomings with regard to facial recognition. Consider whether or not disclosure of prosopagnosia is a good option for your child. Realistically, given that it has not been until recently that the prevalence of prosopagnosia has been understood, it may be some years before sufficient information about the impact of early disclosure, if chosen, will be gathered. Your wise guidance will be important. Teach your child strategies for coping with preventing recognition problems (either by telling people about prosopagnosia, if appropriate and safe to do so, and/or by helping him to look for effective non-facial clues or to learn some polite ways for coping with non-recognition) or provide ideas for coping with embarrassing situations (such as not recognizing a friend or a friend's mom or one's own mom) that will enable him to handle the situation with confidence and dignity and, if necessary, humor. Helping your child to deal well with errors and to see them as "learning opportunities" is crucial. Eventually, he will be able to communicate sensitively regarding the identity errors that he is bound to make, and to keep his sense of self-esteem despite them. There may be a bit of trial and error at first, and this is to be expected. He'll learn. Encourage the development of skills relevant to communicating effectively and sensitively with others.

Helping your child to get his social needs met is important, as in terms of Maslow's "sense of belonging" stage. It may be difficult for a prosopagnosic child to develop a sense of belonging to a group when, in fact, he is having difficulty keeping track as to who the group members are. Make sure that he has the opportunity to spend time developing meaningful interactions that can lead to friendships. You may sometimes need to be proactive in creating play opportunities for him outside of school. If Johnny cannot recognize "Bill" at the end of the school day, how will he be able to invite Bill to his home? You may need to be proactive in helping to find Bill (and his parent or caregiver) to invite him over to play.

If you, as a parent, also have prosopagnosia, you may be able to enlist the teacher's help in alerting you as to the location of Bill's parent, for example. Fostering social learning opportunities for your child by helping to arrange play dates, if he is withdrawn but wishes to play with others, may help to build lifelong social skills while forming friendships. Ideas could include, for example, having him invite others to your house for fun dinners, bake-offs, time in the sandbox, or to explore a particular hobby or interest. Experiment with one-on-one play dates as well as having groups of friends over. See what works and act accordingly in the future. But also respect your child's need for solitude; and address his individual needs.

Be wise about play group structure and size, so that your child's opportunities to meet others, recognize them, and form deep friendships will be successful. Some prosopagnosic children thrive better one on one; others are able to do well in small groups, while still others do just fine in larger groups. Discover what works. Keep in touch. Find out whether the activities are meaningful.

Prepare your child to cope with non-recognition incidents, because the social consequences of failing to recognize others can be significant, and it will benefit him to minimize that negative impact. If people feel snubbed or consistently misunderstood (if the prosopagnosic does not recognize emotional expressions either)—and sighted people are expected to recognize faces and others *do* feel snubbed if not greeted—this can lead to misunderstandings that detract from healthy relationships. Strive to prevent this, if at all possible.

Teach your child to be socially appropriate. If he talks incessantly because he doesn't see the "I'm bored" look, teach him to take frequent "station breaks" and to check in with listeners. Do not simply let him talk on and on for a half hour at a time. It is important that the prosopagnosic learns to get along with others in groups, and most people dislike listening to endless monologues.

If your child has other bad habits that would cause significant discomfort for others—for example, he talks with his mouth full—make sure to teach him to refrain from doing so. Peers and others will be reluctant to teach him manners that you should instill, and it is doing him no favor to ignore maladaptive behavior that will ultimately isolate him.

Consider getting a book for yourself on how to teach manners, or a book on manners that is age appropriate for your child and includes many of the unwritten rules. Without constantly criticizing him, pay attention to how he interacts with others. Teach him to be sensitive, when and how it is age and context appropriate for you to do so.

Lacking facial recognition skills can be embarrassing, and the impending consequences may have an impact on self-esteem. Additionally, lack of confidence with regard to face recognition issues, in terms of classroom group activities, parties, and social activities may further threaten confidence. Help your child learn what to expect and to cope with it when it happens.

Find the areas in which your child excels. Sometimes prosopagnosics are pioneers in their fields or otherwise highly successful professionals. Include your child by developing an atmosphere of understanding and kindness. Teach him to create supportive environments by navigating the social world with grace, and you will provide him with important lifelong skills.

Instill in your child a sense of self-acceptance while building talent.


## AT SOCIAL GATHERINGS

There are many ways in which to support your child during social gatherings at your home. When hosting a gathering, talk about who will be coming prior to their arrival. In addition, whether hosting or attending an event, realize that, if everyone is wearing similar clothes (e.g. if all of the men are wearing similar suits), your prosopagnosic child may not recognize people—even if they are relatives whom he dearly loves. It is nothing personal.

Use people's names as often as possible: "Hi, Aunt Linda" or "Oh, Uncle Bob, thank you for bringing these delicious brownies," instead of a simple, "Hi, how are you?", "Nice to see you!" or "Glad you made it!" If at all possible—and sufficiently appropriate, and the child knows how to read—include name tags at large reunion events. (This is helpful for prosopagnosics of any age for those events at which there will be many "unfamiliar" friends.) Understandably, this will be socially awkward for most situations, however.

You might help your child to understand how to "fish" for information about the person to whom he is talking, by explaining the kinds of socially appropriate questions to ask that will elicit identity information. For example, one may make small talk by asking such questions as "Great party, huh?" "The cake is great! Who made it?" or "Isn't this wonderful music?" In addition, tag questions (statements that end with a question) can be helpful: "It's a beautiful day, isn't it?" Simple comments, such as "Did you have a good flight?" can be inappropriate if the addressee to the comment lives in the same town. Keeping the questions extremely general when identity is uncertain (and disclosure has not occurred) is a useful skill to learn.

A photograph of Uncle Steve taken in December may not help some prosopagnosic children wishing to recognize Uncle Steve at a later date. Experiment to determine what works for your child. If he benefits from seeing gestures, for example, you might want to consider showing a brief video before a family gathering.

Nowadays, you can use digital cameras to take a few photos. Then you may opt to discreetly bring the child into a private area of the house and point out some of the people whom he will see: "Here's Aunt Bella, there's Uncle Bob. Uncle Bob is wearing a blue suit and yellow shirt today." The pictures will show the individuals in the clothes that they will be wearing on the actual day of the party. This may be helpful. Be careful, however, if you do this just before the party starts—do not miss it because you are sitting in a side room for too long. Also realize that photos only help some prosopagnosics. In addition, a party should be just that—a party, a fun social event—and not a stressful "who's who" two-hour exam. Some prosopagnosics are perfectly happy at parties.

Understand that the prosopagnosic child may in some circumstances recognize many people, and it is possible that the recognition may be occurring via clues other than the face. Voice, gesture, body shape, and other non-facial clues may help. While anything is possible (and I will be the first to admit it), do not think that because your child recognizes one person one day, this means that there is no longer a prosopagnosia issue. Be open to possibilities of occurrences beyond what is stated in texts, but also be cautious. Remember: prosopagnosia, itself, was thought to be rare, and it took some courage for those who set up early web pages to be open about their cognovisual difference. Encourage honesty with you, be cautious, realize that texts are supposed to be written to reflect real people—and that real people shouldn't be squeezed in to fit descriptions found in texts. Keep open to the possibility that your child may experience aspects of prosopagnosia not currently described by others who have it.

Be sensitive about whether or not to tell other family members about the recognition issues. Remember: the child is a whole person—with many dimensions to his personality. Let him have fun, flourish, express talent and interests, and discover these in others. Help him to make disclosure decisions—and to determine how, if necessary—regarding the face recognition issues. Navigating the "who to tell" issues, in terms of what is socially appropriate and safe is an important question that needs to be wisely addressed, at home and in school. Comprehending ways in which to do so effectively will be an important, lifelong skill for your child.

Help your child to navigate the social issues related to team sports. Glenn Alperin, who appears to be more severely prosopagnosic than most (he bumps into mirror images of himself in shopping malls) has described on his webpages his own struggle playing sports when growing up. In fact, although he generally advocates against school uniforms, Glenn explains that uniforms are crucial for him when playing sports:

> I discovered very very quickly, when I was younger, that I was not much of an athlete, but, even more importantly, that I could not identify the people on my team unless they were wearing some kind of team uniform. It took the other kids I was playing with even less time to figure out I could not identify who belonged to which teams, and as a result, I was often passing, or throwing, or kicking the ball to the wrong person. The only way I could be even the least bit successful in sports (and that's all I ever was since I wasn't that gifted athletically as I already mentioned) was if people would wear team uniforms to tell me who was on which team. Even in high school, I often had to remind my basketball coach that this was a necessity for me even in scrimmage. (Alperin 2002)

If your child lacks effective identity clues, he may encounter problems regarding, for example, to whom he should throw the ball or who is playing in which position.

Help your child to find social structures that include him effectively. Unless he is highly social, try to minimize the time he spends in huge, amorphous groups in which identity issues will be extremely difficult. If he doesn't want to be highly social, don't constantly force it. Learning to accept and embrace who we are is important in life. Accept your child.

A parent may wish to explore the issue of social risk taking. Is there a way in which to encourage risk taking, even when the possibility of error is fairly high? Is there a way in which to encourage children to feel good about themselves, to gain opportunities to learn identity, even if they are uncertain about the repercussions of the risks? Prosopagnosics have much to learn from those blind people who live adventurous lives and thrive on risk taking. We need to keep in mind, however, that prosopagnosia is a kind of invisible blindness that others may have difficulty understanding, and it could help for the child to have ideas for coping with that challenge, too.

Are your child's talents being tapped? Is there a chance to explore many dimensions of talent, to try art, math, science, poetry, music, and more? Help him to develop self-esteem. Help him to discover, nurture, and contribute talent, to participate in enjoyable activities and offer valuable skill to the community. Teach him self-acceptance and self-confidence, and risk taking. Keep expectations high and believe that he is a smart, contributing, and creative human being.

## WHEN CAREGIVERS ARE PROSOPAGNOSIC TOO

Given the studies that suggest the possibly genetic nature of developmental prosopagnosia (Kennerknecht *et al.* 2006, there is reason to expect that some caregivers, too, will be prosopagnosic.

### Tips for the prosopagnosic parent of a prosopagnosic child

Give your child a way in which to recognize you, and offer him ideas for making himself recognizable to you. Some prosopagnosic parents can visually recognize their children; others cannot. Let your child feel known, understood, and loved.

As previously described, some people will give a child a special code so that he will realize that it is the parent who has driven up and is offering a ride. For example, a special hand gesture, whistle (as Glenn recommended) or password might be helpful. Likewise, your child may also have a code to gesture to you for mutual recognition. If he is too young to use a code, however, you may try dressing him in clothes that are nice as well as appropriate—but distinguishable from those of others.

Similarly for a prosopagnosic parent whose facial recognition is severely impaired, seeing a bunch of bald, look-alike babies all dressed the same when picking up her child at daycare may be confusing. Stitching a little homemade decoration onto your child's onesie, if your own face recognition skills are severely impaired, may be a great way to give yourself a useful recognition clue. Alternatively, you may decide that it is appropriate to disclose your prosopagnosia to the adults in the situation, in which case they may be able to help you at pick-up time. (If you do so, offering this book or details of relevant websites would provide them with some information about prosopagnosia. The growing understanding of its prevalence should result in generally greater public knowledge and empathy for those who have the face recognition deficit.)

If you are hosting or attending a family event that will include people whom neither you nor your child will recognize, consider enlisting the help of a tactful good friend or buddy who will also be at the party. Do not be surprised, however, if the friend is not entirely tactful. It can be difficult at times for "neurotypical" people to understand what prosopagnosics need, and there is much to be said for the kindness of intent.

When hosting, consider inviting manageable groups to your home if your child is extremely uncomfortable with the challenges of meeting large numbers of people. You may consider hosting, for example, a family dinner or small gathering with a few close friends.

Use people's names when you know whom you are talking to. This provides important information for your child.

Comment on what you *do* recognize about people—it makes them feel good. For example, "Aunt Linda, your haircut looks great. When did you get it done?", "Uncle Bob, is that a new jacket?"

Learn to be comfortable in your own skin. Your child may be subconsciously picking up "vibes" from you regarding your own acceptance of your prosopagnosia and your coping with the impairment. Being comfortable with oneself, whatever one's talents—and limitations—is important, prosopagnosic or not, and an important life lesson for children of any age. Prosopagnosic or not, an important gift to give one's child is one's own ability to focus on talents, one's acceptance of limitations, and one's own model of coping with grace.

Chapter 11

# DISCLOSURE OF PROSOPAGNOSIA

Even the most highly confident person of any age will experience times when the admission of prosopagnosia provides a potential source of embarrassment. As has been discussed, recognizing faces is a skill that most have from infancy, and, given the current general lack of public awareness about face recognition deficit, it is understandable that even those willing to listen well to a prosopagnosic who is disclosing may have little understanding as to what to do with that information.

Many prosopagnosics will experience a time during which they will need to decide whether or not to disclose—to tell others—and how many others—and when—about their prosopagnosia. When the issue is faced, there are also related questions to address: Whom should I tell? All of my classmates (or relatives, or later, colleagues) or just a select few? If I only tell a few people, should I divulge this information to those who are "strategically placed" to help me (that is, my teacher or principal) or those to whom I feel the closest, such as my best friend? What will they think about me? Will they tell others? Will I be safe if they do so? Should I tell my friends in Glee Club or risk a non-recognition incident in the cafeteria? If I decide to mention prosopagnosia to my friends, would it be best to do so at the beginning of a relationship, in order to prevent hurt feelings related to non-recognition blunders—or only to those people whom I know well? Will they believe me?

Children less frequently face these questions directly because, as stated earlier, they don't as often realize how different their facial skills are from those around them, and therefore they do not realize that there is anything different to report. Nonetheless, unless a child has figured out ways in which to successfully socialize and acknowledge others, using non-facial strategies, the repercussions of non-recognition may be significant. Certainly, however, understanding the struggles that the prosopagnosic faces with regard to issues of disclosure may help those providing support to gain greater insight into some of the challenges that the child will someday likely confront. As general understanding of prosopagnosia broadens, and more parents become aware of their children's face recognition deficit, the question of disclosure will become an increasingly important one for children and likely more will be known as to the usefulness of disclosing. Rather than have each child individually reinvent the wheel, suggestions as to some of the issues related to "coming out" about prosopagnosia are provided here. Please note that these should be not interpreted as an endorsement for being open about non-recognition, because there is not enough currently known on the subject to endorse the decision, but rather as an offering of ideas as to whether and how to be open, should this path be chosen.

Whom and how to tell is a very individual and personal choice and will certainly be influenced by the prosopagnosic's life circumstances, including those of safety, school and class climate, age, personality, and preferences, as well as the quality and length of relationship with those to whom disclosure is being considered. Sometimes one can cope more effectively by privately addressing the issue, while teachers and caregivers discreetly pitch in by providing identity information, when possible. There may be times, however, during which disclosure can be useful.

Safety is a crucial factor in the decision-making process related to disclosure. Are there many bullies in the school? Is the neighborhood safe? Is the child a latchkey child? These factors should contribute, and obviously, if disclosure would compromise the child's safety, it should be reconsidered.

School and class climate are also important to the disclosure decision. Is there a substantial, strong school community? Is the child likely to gain the support that she needs to foster positive relationships if she comes out? Be realistic here. This isn't about the way that things "should" be, but rather the truth about how things are, the day-to-day, in-and-out questions of whether the school succeeds in nurturing diversity with compassion and respect. Remember that if the child discloses in the third grade, her prosopagnosia will still be known in the tenth. School climate is an important factor in the decision-making process regarding disclosure.

The child's personality is an issue too. Is she one who would be comfortable with others' knowing? Will it help her to thrive better, if others know? Or will it make her extremely uncomfortable?

Does the individual to whom one is considering disclosing need to know? Will this person tell others? If so, would that be acceptable?

Your child can strive to become graceful and smart in navigating the "whom to tell" issues, in terms of what works for her. What may be absolutely appropriate and relevant in one situation—say, a classroom full of students whom she will see daily versus a particular event at which one is less likely to encounter others again—sometimes dictates which decision will be made, so that a prosopagnosic may be open in some situations and not in others.

If the decision is made to disclose, remember that it may not be easy the first time nor the first several times, and it may take a while for your child to determine her "comfort zone." Teaching her to live well with the ambiguities will be one of the important lessons of disclosure, and of prosopagnosia, in general.

## DIFFICULTY OF OTHERS IN RECOGNIZING PROSOPAGNOSIA

In truth, it is important to recall that the widespread prevalence of prosopagnosia is only now beginning to be understood. Some years may need to pass and experiences shared before the best paths to choose, along these lines, or at least the repercussions of each path, are more deeply understood. Consider, for example, the cochlear implant issue described earlier in this book. Making an intuitive decision as a parent, whether or not those decisions reflect the current trends, is sometimes the best path for one to take in responding to one's child's particular needs.

Certainly, if the path of disclosure is chosen, it is reasonable to guess that without excellent guidance for normally sighted children when learning about face recognition deficit, it will likely be difficult for those in your child's life to understand the condition. There are obstacles to others' understanding that will need to be overcome.

### "But she can see!"

Some children (and for that matter, adults) find it difficult to comprehend that, even though the prosopagnosic has two eyes in working order, she is claiming to not be able to recognize people. These non-prosopagnosics need to be educated to the fact that seeing and recognizing are not the same thing: prosopagnosia is related to how the brain processes visual information—and not about what is typically called "eyesight" or visual acuity. Anecdotally, prosopagnosics often report that they have trouble with others' comprehending their recognition issues. When one considers that most people are able to recognize faces within the first several months of life, however, this misunderstanding becomes a bit more "understandable." The prosopagnosic may require empathy, but she will also need to offer it, difficult as that may be sometimes.

## The challenge of empathy

It may be challenging at times for children to put themselves in others' shoes. Understanding prosopagnosia requires that they comprehend a significant, unobvious perceptive difference. I am reminded of a time when I saw a very well-meaning fourth grader "explain" to a blind woman (a teacher in a school) what certain rocks were like by placing the teacher's fingertips on photos of the rocks. The child had seen that Braille helped the woman to understand letters, and he had concluded that similar learning could occur with regard to feeling pictures. The child was trying to be kind, but his understanding of her perception was understandably limited, given his age. Comprehending perceptive difference can be challenging, even for adults, as well as for those children who are well meaning. If the prosopagnosic child in your classroom is open about the face recognition deficit, the other children will need help in understanding what this means.

## "She recognizes Sammy, but she doesn't recognize me."

Because your child may recognize some children, at least some of the time, it may be hard for the other children to understand that she really does not recognize the others. In addition, the prosopagnosic may recognize someone in some contexts, but not in others. This, too, can be difficult for non-prosopagnosics to understand, and, if the child with face recognition deficit lacks an explanation, this can be confusing to those in her life. Given this, if the child is open about the prosopagnosia, it may be helpful to provide her with opportunity to practice articulating responses to these concerns, if they are raised. In fact, some children who disclose may find it useful to have a few practice opportunities for explaining to others that this is common among prosopagnosics, because clues such as hair, clothing, gesture, and context can be helpful and are not always readily available. The reasons why some people are recognizable to a prosopagnosic may vary. It may be that these people have distinctive hair, gait, body shape, context, or one of a number of possible features relevant to the prosopagnosic.

If children in a class *are* told about non-recognition, they need a highly effective leader to build a climate supportive of such difference. They may not know what to do, and, therefore, ideas for *how* to be supportive, in terms of the prosopagnosia, will need to be shared with them. They will need suggestions that are easy to understand and which do not ask too much of them as children. They will need to be able to exercise enough discretion so that the prosopagnosic child feels more a part of the group as a result of the coming out, and not less so. Indeed, sensitively, discreetly including the prosopagnosic child so that she may contribute effectively to the group and be understood by others is a challenge that will require of the teacher both wisdom and skill. Guidance needs to be offered to the class as a whole.

A parent or teacher also needs to be realistic in understanding that even if only a limited group of children are told today, it is likely that the information about the prosopagnosia could follow the child into the schoolyard and throughout her school years. You need to be thoughtful and deliberate in making this decision with your child about whether being open is a good idea at this time.

If parent and prosopagnosic child decide that the child will come out, then the question needs to be addressed as to whom and how? If the child is open, some guidance is probably needed in helping her determine how to get the other children to understand the prosopagnosia question. Depending upon the severity of the prosopagnosia, a teacher may, for example, ask the prosopagnosic child in the lower grades if she might like to try a buddy system that would enable her to have playmates during recess. Consider also whether it would be possible to sensitively strengthen her social opportunities by discussing prosopagnosia issues with the class. Even if the child does not disclose, the adults in her life can nonetheless use many previously described strategies to provide support.

## DISCLOSURE STRATEGIES

This list is by no means complete, but rather a suggestion of possibilities for ways of disclosing, and the individual child as well as the specific people involved in the presentation or conversation are important in determining what would be appropriate. Indeed, as varied strategies are practiced over time, it will become clear as to which ideas are the most helpful. If any are tried, it should be with an open mind and the awareness that they may or may not prove fruitful. "Recoup and regroup" may be necessary.

If you do talk with other children about your child's prosopagnosia, it may be useful to have a coloring or story book that highlights differences related to hair and clothes (common characteristics that help prosopagnosics to identify others) that will introduce the children to the topic. Make the discussion fun, interesting, and relevant.

The following suggestions include ideas for the kind of information that would be helpful for your child to provide to other children, as well as a sample conversation.

Please note that in cases where there are examples of dialogues that can take place, these are provided as examples. You and/or your child may have a way in which to express yourself that is more appropriately suited to your personality and your child's—and the other individual's—needs.

## One-on-one, child to child

The prosopagnosic child, or the child and parent together, talk with the non-prosopagnosic child, or that child and her parent, to let them know that it is a lot of fun to play together but that the prosopagnosic child wants to tell about a problem that sometimes makes it hard to recognize people. However, if the friend could kindly say "Hi" first and the prosopagnosic child hears the friend's voice, for instance, it would be easier. And if the prosopagnosic child ever doesn't say "Hi," the non-prosopagnosic should not take offense, because it is nothing personal. (Prosopagnosia is not a "visual" problem per se, and it may be a challenge for a child to discuss that it is a cognitive one, but, if pressed, the child could perhaps say that face recognition deficit is related to how the brain enables the child to see.)

EXAMPLE

The child, or the child and parent together, talk with the non-prosopagnosic child, or that child and her parent, and say something to the effect of, "I really have fun playing with you a lot. I just want to tell you that I have a problem that sometimes makes it hard for me to recognize people. So if you say "Hi" to me first and I hear your voice [or other relevant attribute], it will be easier. And if I ever don't say "Hi," if you could let me know, that would be great. I may not recognize you."

## One-on-one, parent to parent

The parent of the prosopagnosic child may speak with the parent of the non-prosopagnosic in order to inform the other of the facial recognition deficit and to ask for support, if needed. This may provide a strategy enabling both parents to keep an eye out for potential problems so that, if the non-prosopagnosic child is inadvertently not recognized, the parent can provide a ready explanation that will lead to understanding. In fact, the parent of the "neurotypical child" may then speak one-on-one with their child to come up with strategies for being supportive to the prosopagnosic, just as the prosopagnosic would be taught to be supportive of the other, if need be, in other circumstances.

SAMPLE SCRIPT

> Tommy (prosopagnosic) really enjoys playing with your child a great deal. Please understand that he has some challenges, a cogniovisual issue called prosopagnosia. Basically, this means that he has a face recognition deficit. You can look it up online, if you'd like. He doesn't recognize people by the face, and so there may be instances where he may not recognize Robbie outside of context.
>
> Anything that your child can do to help out by initiating a conversation when that happens would be very helpful. If Tommy hears Robbie's voice or if Robbie mentions an activity that they have recently done together—for example, "That was a fun game of chess yesterday, Tommy." [or whichever recognition strategies work for the child]— he'll be likely to recognize you and Robbie in that way. I know that he so enjoys playing with Robbie very much. And by the way, if he inadvertently fails to say hello to your child at any point, it would be great if you could help Robbie to understand.

## Child to class

(This is for that rare, exceptionally sensitive teacher, who can pull this off and make it work.)

There are some rare, exceptionally sensitive and skillful teachers who can pull off developing a class climate that is so supportive as to enable a child to successfully talk to the class about a special issue, whether it be blindness, hearing impairment, or, in this case, prosopagnosia. If this strategy is used, the child can speak with the class, for example, in a circle group, and describe what prosopagnosia is, as well as provide an opportunity for others to ask questions, so that it becomes a true learning opportunity for other students. The advantage of this approach is that it can provide a chance for the prosopagnosic child to learn to give information about her impairment, and to clarify what it actually is in a meaningful way that will engage their attention. It can be a great learning opportunity for everyone.

The child and teacher, with the permission and support of a parent, would need to be comfortable with this approach, and guidance from the teacher in helping the other children to understand how to be supportive of the prosopagnosic child might be required. In a special way, however, this can be an opportunity for the prosopagnosic child to shine, to begin to feel comfortable with—rather than embarrassed about—the difference. If the class climate is less than excellent, however, the disclosure could result in the child's being made fun of or excluded from activities. This should be absolutely avoided, and other strategies used instead, if at all, if it is suspected that exclusion would result. In addition, one would need to keep in mind that others' knowledge of the face recognition deficit could follow the child throughout her school years.

If this approach is taken, the teacher should be ready to look out for misunderstanding among students, and to jump in to correct it, if necessary. And if exclusion does result, then a quick "recoup and regroup" would need to take place to turn things around. If it works, however, the opportunity could be wonderful.

SAMPLE SCRIPT

> I have a visual issue which is a face recognition deficit. It's called pros-opagnosia. It means that I have a lot of difficulty with recognizing people. I can sometimes know you by (fill in the blanks with your child's recognition strategies)—that is, your voice, your clothes, your —and so if you help me to understand who you are, it's much easier for me. If you come up to me if you want to play, that would be great.
>
> Teacher: Thank you, Melinda, that's very interesting, and it helps us to understand you. Okay, now, does anybody have any questions for Melinda? If so, Melinda will answer your questions. One at a time, please. (Then the teacher points to each person while saying their names. "Yes, Robbie? What is your question for Melinda?")

## Teacher to elementary class (with child's and parent's permission)

Under some circumstances it may be useful for a teacher to talk with an elementary school class about the topic. The advantages are that the teacher may have the language and knowledge of the other students to assure that all understand, and a more authoritative tone can be taken, if at times necessary, in addressing the issue. She may also be able to recognize lack of understanding and quickly correct this among students. There can be a follow-up with questions that the teacher, the prosopagnosic student, and/or both can answer. The teacher needs to be clear about identifying ways in which others can be supportive of their classmate.

Consider also whether it would be possible, with sensitivity, to strengthen the child's social opportunities by discussing prosopagnosia issues with the class.

SAMPLE SCRIPT

> I would like to talk with you about something important. Now, Tommy is a very wonderful boy, as you all know, he's our friend, isn't he, and his seeing may appear to be normal. Have any of you met a blind person? (Call on students)… Well, Tommy isn't blind, but he has a visual problem, that means, a problem with seeing. Even though he can see people, it is hard for him to recognize people. Have any of you ever had trouble recognizing people? (Raise hands and discuss) Well, that is often the case for Tommy. He may recognize your hair color or your clothes or your hat. Now, I want everyone to be helpful and nice about this. When you see Tommy, please say hello to him (add here other strategies that may help Tommy), because he will recognize your voice. Does anyone have any other ideas?

Sensitively educate the other children about prosopagnosia so that they can learn to be friends to the prosopagnosic child. This could make life much easier for everyone, as the other children understand that they may need to say hello first and hint or indicate as to their names.

## Who, exactly, should know?

Whether to tell everyone in the class, just a few select friends, or no-one is an important question.

Remember that even if a student discloses her prosopagnosia to others, it will still be important to navigate the "who to tell—when to tell" issue at times. There will be instances when the prosopagnosia will not be of interest to the other party, in much the same way as when a little known neighbor asks "How are you doing?" she doesn't really want to know about the details of our intimate health issues and financial woes. Understanding whom to tell, when, and how to do so in a manner that the other party can comprehend is an important lifelong skill that can have an impact on future relationships. Your offering the child ideas so that she does not have to "reinvent the wheel" and navigate all of these questions "solo" can be helpful.

## WHAT OTHER CHILDREN CAN DO TO HELP

It is a good idea when beginning the disclosure journey to set high expectations—but recognize that it is likely to be an imperfect one, and that's okay. Many learning journeys require risk and education from trial and error—and this is one without many maps—and with the child, parent, teacher, and, in some cases, other childcare professional(s) as captain. Realize that you may need to switch gears. For example, you and your child may think that one approach will help her to feel comfortable, but in the end it doesn't. Be ready to adapt, dust yourself off, and move on. Keep working until you are successful.

In terms of finding ways in which other children—and adults—can be helpful, realize that not all prosopagnosic children are comfortable with the same strategies, and in fact some children may not know what they are comfortable with until they have tried a few. Find out what works best for your child. Help her to feel comfortable with the ambiguity, while she discovers and then settles for what works.

## How other children can be helpful

Other children can help your child by introducing themselves and interacting with the prosopagnosic child. It would be particularly helpful if the interaction included information that would help the prosopagnosic to narrow down who the speaker is: "Hi, Tommy, that was a lot of fun playing catch yesterday after school." They can say hello and add in activities in which they have participated with the child recently: "Hi, Linda, it was fun playing house during free time today."

Some prosopagnosic children may find a direct introduction (e.g. "Hi, Mary, it's me, Bob") to be quite comfortable and helpful, while others feel that such directness, uncommon among other children, makes them "stick out like a sore thumb" and is therefore inadvisable. Find what works for your child through wise consideration, trial and error—and check in. Your child's needs may change as she develops.

Other children can simply say hello, "Hi, Mary," particularly if your child is good at voice recognition. And while for some this is sufficient, if Mary doesn't recognize some facial expressions, at times the hello may be a bit startling because there may not be an opportunity to recognize that she is about to be greeted. While for most people the hello is expected following an expression of recognition, for that group of prosopagnosic children who do not see emotional expressions, the greeting may be surprising—or even a bit jarring. You might teach your child to gracefully respond to this. (Please be careful regarding her safety. Remember that not everyone who knows her name will necessarily be a "friend" to her.)

Children can include the prosopagnosic child in games and lunch activities: "Come on, do you want to sit with us?" "Want to look for frogs?"

As previously mentioned, a coloring book, story book, or coloring activity that emphasizes hair and clothes can be helpful. Talk with the children so that they will understand how important hair color, clothing, etc. can be to the prosopagnosic child.

## What other children need to know if the prosopagnosic child discloses

"Mary likes you; she just sometimes doesn't recognize you."

"Mary may sometimes be shy to approach you, but you might try approaching her."

"You should invite Mary to play with you at recess time."

"Be nice, but sometimes you may need to be direct with Mary (if Mary doesn't recognize emotional expressions). You can tell her how you feel."

This last suggestion needs the guidance of an adult, because children may at times need to be direct, but in a way that is fair. Prosopagnosics who fail to recognize emotional expressions may have problems with comprehending another's irritation or boredom, for example, without explicit information, fairly delivered.

Creating an atmosphere in which children are accepting of difference is an important challenge and a useful life commitment to instill.

## Buddy systems

Sometimes encouraging student-to-student support is a wonderful way in which to address student needs, and yet how to do so without causing discomfort, so that the diversity in the classroom strengthens classroom ties, is a delicate and important question. A formal buddy system could pose the risk of embarrassment for the prosopagnosic child, and this is an important consideration, as one wishes to bolster the child's self-esteem, not weaken it. A worthwhile tactic for gaining identity help for the child might be to discuss with the parent and (depending upon the parent's response) the child as to whether there is a close friend in the class who can be asked to sometimes informally provide identity information. If so, then that child's friend may be asked as to whether she would be willing to sometimes discreetly provide that information. Likely the greatest challenge, if this is tried, will be to informally educate the buddy as to how to be both helpful and tactful in offering relevant, timely identity information. This is a tall order for a child; even well meaning adults sometimes have trouble with understanding how to discretely offer pertinent identity information to prosopagnosic friends. Given the need for inclusion, autonomy, and self-esteem, any kind of disclosure – including informal disclosure such as this – requires caution and thought.

On the other hand, the idea of a more formal buddy system is to provide a friend in the classroom who will work with the child and offer information that is not readily available. This will be particularly helpful if the child is in a classroom of many students. As is the case with all of the topics listed, formal buddy systems need to be considered carefully; their success will depend not only upon the individual prosopagnosic child and other children in the class, but also upon the school and class climate, in general. In most cases, formal buddy systems are not recommendable, as they will single out the prosopagnosic child. However, a more formal system might work in a classroom in which all of the other students also have buddies. In such a case, the help of the buddy could informally (within the context of the formal system) be enlisted, and the prosopagnosic child could be provided with support.

If the buddy system can be created in a manner that will help the prosopagnosic child, nurture an equal (rather than dependent) relationship, and operate smoothly, so as to offer information to the prosopagnosic without distracting or disrupting the class, such a system may be a way of getting relevant information to the child without too much planning, although the buddy may need information before starting, delivered one-on-one, and with discreet, private check-ins along the way. In turn, the buddy learns responsibility, the children see a model of partnership, and, hopefully, if the prosopagnosic child has opportunity to reciprocate her talent in other ways, depending upon who the prosopagnosic child and buddies are, such a system can help both children—and the classroom—to thrive. The buddy needs to know the specific information related to *when* the prosopagnosic will need her and what, exactly, to do, as well as *how* to do it respectfully. If such a system occurs within a class that uses a general buddy system for other children, too, there can be much to be gained. This is important, and so to clarify here: a buddy system should not be a kind of "babysitting" system, but rather a structure for an equal partnership that enables the prosopagnosic child to get information to which she lacks access, and offers opportunity for the prosopagnosic child to share talent (which will vary, depending upon the child) with the buddy.

Have the buddy offhandedly and naturally sprinkle in other people's names when talking, and explicitly teach the buddy to act kindly and gracefully, if necessary, while also thanking and celebrating her for her contributions. (Teach the prosopagnosic child to do this.)

Check in privately with the prosopagnosic child to assure that her needs are being met through the buddy system. Do not simply ask, "Are things okay with your buddy?" The child may not know how to answer or articulate if things are not going well. Rather, ask specific questions that will elicit answers to provide you with satisfactory and relevant information: for example, "What kinds of things are you and your buddy doing together? Can you tell me about that? Do you like it?"

Remember also that there are specific times of the day when the child could benefit from a buddy, particularly when people are moving around in a manner that is unstructured and unpredictable, such as during lunch time or in the school yard.

Keep in mind too that a highly effective buddy system may at a later time need to be changed or eliminated. One needs to pay attention to changing circumstances.

An alternative to a buddy system, if you feel that a buddy system will single the child out too much, would be to have all children partner between classes, when moving from class to class. It is a challenge sometimes in teaching for the educator to meet the individual needs of one child in specific ways while also addressing the needs—both individual and general—of the larger group. Determine how to best structure your class in a manner that will most effectively accomplish these goals.

A buddy system, perhaps for all or some childern, could be useful during recess. You may, for example, ask the prosopagnosic child and others if they might like to try a buddy system that would enable them to have friends to play with during recess, whether or not such a system is used during regular class time hours. If the buddy system is used during both class time and recess, a different buddy may be used for each—or buddies may be regularly changed. (Please recall that there are alternative ideas to buddy systems for recess time offered in Chapter 7.)

Remember, in introducing the buddy to this opportunity of friendship, to bring it up matter-of-factly. Make prosopagnosia seem natural (it is).

The prosopagnosic student should not be made to feel like a "child" among peers. The buddy system will not work for all students and, if it simply isn't working, bring it to an end. The goal should be to provide an additional vehicle to help the child to "belong." If this goal is not being met, then reconsider having the system. Keep in touch with the child and her parent about this.

Buddy systems for older children and teens are different from those for younger children, given the importance of independence and sense of belonging that teens often experience, and such systems should be made with care, while including the teen in the decision making. She should not "feel stupid" or "out of place," and, as is the case with younger children, serious consideration should be given to an alternative strategy if there is discomfort with a buddy system. That having been said, ways of finding a buddy for a teen will likely need to be different from strategies used for a younger child. Another teen with similar interests might be informally told about the prosopagnosia and taught strategies for including the other in conversations, for example.

## IDEAS FOR SUPPORTING THE PROSOPAGNOSIC CHILD (AS VIEWED THROUGH THE LENS OF MASLOW'S THEORY)

### Physiological

In a way that respects the child's dignity, ensure that there are ways in which she will be able to get her physiological and safety needs met. Make sure that she has ways in which to recognize you. Offer her a code if her face recognition skills are so impaired as to require this. Keep on the lookout for bullying.

### Social (love, belonging)

Ensure that the child has ways in which to form healthy relationships with others. Consider group sizes and structures that will enable her to truly stretch socially. As is the case with all children, the opportunity to explore interests and hobbies can be a wonderful way to get to know others more intimately. Teach her to communicate effectively and to elicit information verbally that may not be available facially.

### Self-esteem

Find areas of talent so that the child can develop them. Also, consider helping her to feel comfortable in her own skin, accepting herself as a complete and worthy person, prosopagnosic or not. Come up with ideas for minimizing and coping with identity errors, once she gets old enough to worry about this.

Consider the impact that disclosure would have on self-esteem. Given the context of the child's personality, social skills, school, and neighborhood environment, would disclosure help or hinder the goals of her better fitting in?

Prosopagnosics are sometimes highly successful in the areas of their disciplines. Given this, it is important to remember not to focus on the deficit, but rather to use your understanding of it to bolster ways in which the child will be able to develop social understanding, while developing and thriving in many other ways.

## Self-actualization

Help the growing child to discover, express, and contribute to society in ways that are personally meaningful and socially relevant.

Chapter 12

# FACIAL EXPRESSIONS
# AND PROSOPAGNOSIA

## IDENTITY GATHERING, SOCIAL UNDERSTANDING, AND FACIAL EXPRESSIONS

For most people, faces are the hook on which to "hang" information about others' lives, interests, preferences, style, status, and more. Recognizing faces and emotional expressions enables us to:

- gather knowledge about others

- make it possible to predict social behaviour

- comprehend how words and actions have different impacts on lives

- understand the constellations of behavior that may please, excite, annoy, disappoint, endear, and more.

That is, facial identification and the perception of emotional facial expressions offer access to the various patterns of character that make each person unique, enabling us to respond to others' unstated need, as we come to know them.

If I know that Sharon doesn't like loud music, I'll be careful not to play it when I'm around her—but I need to first be able to identify who Sharon is and—importantly, to comprehend her facial expressions, if she doesn't verbally articulate her discomfort with my actions. If I don't recognize Sharon at all, and she has told me before not to play the loud music, I might not act considerately—and Sharon may not realize that I lack the choice. Eventually, if this happens frequently enough, I may be excluded from some social activities, and this lack of practice may impact my ability to optimally develop social understanding.

Eventually, these layers of information enable us to become sensitive to others' needs, to make wise decisions as we negotiate the complex social world in which we live. If Courtney always sees Bob and Dave together, she may not be surprised that a quarrel with Bob might also result in Dave's being annoyed, even if Dave is not present during the quarrel. Or, if she realizes that Ellie is the child who always carries her favorite doll or truck, she may decide that a new hat for the doll or another truck would make a great birthday present. The culmination of multiple events, which enables us to glean information about who others are, adds to our understanding as we reflect about the world. Ultimately, this enables us to become more socially astute.

Regardless of what our information hook is, it is important that we are able to gather information, to build on what we know about people, to comprehend the various patterns that make each person unique, and to recognize the possible effects of our behavior on others. To put it simply, it appears that a child's ability to recognize faces and facial expressions can influence others' interactions with him; ultimately, this will influence his opportunities for social learning. What begins as a physical response to a real cognovisual phenomenon ultimately becomes a psychosocial one as the child develops.

Face recognition and the perception of emotional expression, what will be called here "emocioperception", will influence ability to form friendships, predict behavior, know what to say, to whom, and when, and determine many more behaviors. In other words, identity information, and particularly the ability to comprehend another's emotional experience, will help a child to develop social understanding or what has been called "social intelligence." Compounding the problem for those who have difficulty recognizing some or many facial expressions is the suggestion, (Lindner and Rosen 2006) according to some research related to Asperger syndrome, that the ability to visually identify facial expressions appears to correlate with ability—or impairment—in comprehending emotional information from tone of voice and other vocal qualities or "prosody." In other words, while a blind person can usually gather emotional information and develop understanding accordingly by hearing how a person expresses himself with his voice, the prosopagnosic who has what will be called here "emociagnosia"—inability to recognize some of the broad spectrum of emotional facial expressions—might also miss the aural cues, if this research is correct. Thus, an individual who lacks ability to comprehend intonation may hear a voice get louder—but fail to hear the anger or excitement being communicated. If there is a correlation between difficulty comprehending facial emotional expressions and difficulty processing emotion as conveyed by the voice, then this would suggest that opportunities to comprehend another's emotional experience—unless people are explicitly clear (and the prosopagnosic is able to handle that explicit information)—could be limited.

## EMOTIONAL EXPRESSIONS

### The perception of emotional expressions

A child's social world expands even during infancy; however, it has become clear that not all children—or adults—prosopagnosic or not, develop the ability to recognize emotional expressions efficiently. Dr. Paul Ekman, who has spent years studying the meaning of facial expressions, has turned the art of intuiting emotions into a kind of science, and he has concluded that the meaning of facial expressions across cultures is universal. Wherever one goes in the world, people's facial expressions mean basically the same thing, and whether the individual is a member of a nomadic tribe in a deep forest or a business person passing through the "jungles" of Wall Street, expressing, for example, excitement, loss, or joy, the facial expressions displayed when the individual is alone and has the privacy to express real emotion are basically the same. That is, private emotions, it appears, are the same across cultures, and they will be expressed similarly on the face—even though public displays of feeling may vary somewhat depending upon the culture, according to the research (Ekman 2003) what is appropriate in a particular culture can influence our learning to mask some emotions. However, as Ekman (2003) has also noted in his book, *Emotions Revealed*, we are not all equal in our ability to interpret what those particular facial expressions mean. In other words, while the meaning of facial expressions is universal, our ability to comprehend them is not. In fact, an internet search using the key words "recognize emotional facial expressions" will reveal studies being done even now that show how into our adult lives there are many factors that influence our accuracy in interpreting facial expressions.

While some prosopagnosics can recognize a broad range of emotional expressions, including the six basic expressions that the scientist, Charles Darwin (1987), described in his work along with those far more subtle, other prosopagnosics may not even see all of the main six—happiness, sorrow, fear, disgust, anger, and surprise. Other prosopagnosics may see the main six and miss the more complex expressions, the shades of feeling that may mean the difference between, for example, "happiness combined with excitement" and "happiness combined with surprise and confusion." Still others may recognize emotional expressions with some efficiency.

## The importance of recognizing emotional expressions

> If emotional expressions were background music, what would be the soundtrack of your life? It's not what the lips, eyes, or mouth look like; it's what they do: curve up, grin sarcastically, sneakily hide information, tell everything, suppress laughter. The many simple and complex expressions that ultimately convey character are important to recognition for those prosopagnosics able to see facial expressions, become, in a sense, a kind of soundtrack, but visual in nature.

Understanding facial expressions helps a sighted child to form close bonds, comprehend intention, predict others' actions, and pick up cues that provide warning of a need to alter—or continue—a behavior. Looks of boredom may inform the child that it is time to "stop talking," expressions of anger should in some cases lead to the speaker's ceasing a particular action—or starting one, a look of sorrow may compel someone to offer help or comfort, or one of happiness may urge another to continue doing something. Understanding others' facial expressions provides information crucial to navigating the world of human relationships.

While some children—(and particularly those on the autistic spectrum as some theorists suggest)—tend to lack ability in this regard, others find it an area of strength, and indeed the ability to recognize emotional facial expressions may enable some prosopagnosics to socialize very effectively.

Comprehending facial expressions can be useful to a prosopagnosic in the following ways:

## Determining identity

A prosopagnosic with strong emocioperception ability can understand that an acquaintance who is generally sorrowful or mischievous may have a look that conflicts with any verbal expressions of happiness, for example.

Most people have specific combinations of facial expressions that they frequently subconsciously exhibit, and which typify their character. Understanding aspects of character conveyed by facial expressions can contribute to identifying others and also build on social understanding in general. If one knows that two people look similar but usually express different constellations of emotions, their facial expressions may help the prosopagnosic who recognizes emotional expressions well to distinguish between these people, even if subconsciously so. For example, if there are two long-haired, brunette receptionists who work at the office, but one receptionist almost always smiles and the other does not, this expression can provide a useful hint to the prosopagnosic who can see it. Indeed, one theory is that the physical motion of the face itself may provide identity clues to the prosopagnosic.

## Recognizing the "hello look"

Prosopagnosics who see the expression of recognition that almost always precedes a greeting, or what may be called "the hello look," will know when they are being recognized, and this can encourage them to initiate a conversation with others. They can often mingle comfortably at parties, whether or not exact identity is known, and basically they are able to socialize, participate in, and thrive on social events. In fact, even if the prosopagnosic does not initially recognize the conversant, facial expressions noticed (even subconsciously) may "jog" the memory, enabling him to determine identity—at times, within minutes or seconds. Those who recognize facial expressions well have access to information that may quickly lead to conversation that can offer important identity clues.

## Acting in friendship, bonding

In a sense, emotional expression, whether conveyed by the face, voice, touch, or words (as in the case of deaf or blind people who sometimes communicate verbally through letters signed into each other's hands) is the notation of social understanding, leading to friendship, and having an impact on all human relationships. Facial expressions enable the seer to understand others' non-verbally communicated intentions. Whether a child can see someone happily playing a game or looking annoyed about it, emotional expressions carry important information in the social interaction. If a friend says, "I'm feeling great," but looks and/or sounds sad, one can respond to this.

## Picking up unspoken cues

Children can also pick up on unspoken cues regarding how others would like them to act, and then choose to alter their behavior. If an individual states, "I am very happy about doing this with you," but his emotional expressions conflict with this statement, a prosopagnosic with strong ability to perceive facial expressions can perceive the conflict and alter his behavior—or, simply, understand the individual and build social understanding—accordingly.

## PROFESSIONALLY ADDRESSING ISSUES OF EMOCIAGNOSIA

The many challenges facing those with limited ability to perceive facial expressions are sometimes addressed with thoughtful guidance, as professionals work to help a child glean information by using non-facial strategies or to strengthen his perceptive ability in this area. Professionals, including speech therapists, special needs teachers, and/or child psychologists, among others, may use methods such as "pragmatics" and/or technology systems designed to help children comprehend the meaning of emotional facial expressions and to track improvement of this skill. As new books and videos are constantly coming out on such topics, a parent may wish to do an Amazon, Google, or YouTube search using such key words as "learn emotional expressions" or "pragmatics." Keep in mind, however, that as one speech therapist has noted, it may be years before professionals actually comprehend the long-term consequences—including usefulness—of the exercises on offer, some of which are quite new. In addition, tests designed to determine a child's understanding of facial expressions may "get at" her ability to comprehend them "on paper," but not in authentic situations. Gaining fluency in the language of emotional expressions, as in any language, requires moving beyond the test until the understanding is so ingrained as to become intuitive.

## PROGRAMS

There are many books and programs that offer ideas for teaching social skills and for practicing responding to social events without a child's having full access to emotional expression. An internet search for "pragmatics" or "pragmatics worksheets" will provide useful ideas on this topic.

Increasingly, software and other programs are being developed to provide children with practice at comprehending social information communicated via the face and voice. Such programs as "Mind reading" offer children a chance to practice by viewing and listening to real actors, playing games that test their skills, etc. Other programs, such as "Transporters" and "Gaining face," also aim to teach emotional expressions and may be found by an internet search using keywords such as "emotional expressions autism software." It is challenging for a parent or professional to determine ahead of time whether any—or all—of these programs will be effective for a child. Doing research prior to purchase can include communicating with those who have tried the programs, by looking at such reviews as those on Amazon or inquiring in online discussion groups as to whether any members have any feedback regarding the programs. Whether or not your child is on the autistic spectrum, you may be able to find others who have tried the programs by searching for discussion groups on topics such as special needs, autism, and Asperger syndrome. Asking for samples, and confirming guarantees regarding program quality ahead of time, are important. Make sure that you have determined a way in which to measure progress prior to starting a program, and remember that while persisting despite a setback is often important, it is also crucial to be able to move to a different activity if something is simply not working.

No program should be a child's "entire world." Make sure to spend time on supporting his talents and pleasures. Remember that childhood is a very neurologically fertile period. Provide many tools to enable your child to thrive, to develop talent, to joyfully and creatively explore areas in which he is naturally successful—even if you, as parent or professional—do not necessarily have strength or interest in those areas.

## GAINING EMOTIONAL INFORMATION NON-FACIALLY

Understanding the information that a child is missing is crucial to offering relevant strategies that have an effective impact on learning. It appears that the prosopagnosic child who misses emotional facial expressions will benefit by gaining important social information in non-facial ways. Therefore, it is useful to determine as to whether the prosopagnosic child can see the subtleties of emotional facial expressions.

Supporters may consider teaching the child to sensitively elicit explicit emotional information from others and to cope gracefully with that information when it is negative, and also to pause during conversations, in order to leave space in conversations that will offer others the room in which to speak. They may also coach him to elicit explicit information by asking such questions as "What do you think?" or "This is interesting, isn't it?" during conversations—that is, to use a teaching term, to "dipstick" for understanding or interest. Educate the child to discover information not readily available, guide him to clearly show interest in and understand others' feelings by asking relevant questions. It may be useful to teach a young child who fails to recognize the main emotional expressions to cope with the inevitable issues and social conflicts that will occur. For example, if there is an outburst that the child has not seen coming (due to missed expressions of irritation that have gradually developed into outright anger), he needs to know how to kindly but clearly respond, elicit details, and express to others a desire to address their needs while respecting his own. He may also require the intervention of an adult in helping playmates to be understanding. This is a tall order for a person of any age.

Some professionals may try such strategies as showing brief videos and eliciting information about turn taking during conversations, role playing involving a child's trying to interrupt *you* while you offer a monologue, or teaching him to use tag questions such as "This is a good game, isn't it?" or direct questions such as "How do you like this movie? I'm getting a little bored, aren't you?"

It may help for the supporter to try to offer the child explicit emotional information, to keep the child "in the loop" and well practiced at responding to information about others' feelings. For example, instead of simply saying, "Thank you for the flowers," a parent may say, if it is true, "I was really feeling down before. It really made me happy to receive such a thoughtful gift. Thank you." Instead of simply saying, "I'm getting a headache from all of your nagging," say, "I feel upset when I hear people asking me for things all the time, it makes me tired and frustrated, because I can't or won't always provide those things. I need you to stop." In a positive light, the parent may say, "I feel so happy to see you content, and you've been really inventive about using your time well today. I know that you've been inside all day today, but you've really been patient, and that makes me quite happy."

It is important to give the child rules for social behavior so that he will be able to thrive in communities in a manner socially appropriate. In addition, it may be useful for an adult who can comprehend emotional expressions to sensitively, discreetly, and tactfully serve as interpreter at times, to help the child understand the missed signs.

To an extent, the child's coping in the social arena will require not only his own patience and effort, but also the same on the part of members of the community, because they will at times be required to become somewhat more explicit than usual, and to find ways in which to do so politely and comfortably.

# Chapter 13

# DIAGNOSIS OF PROSOPAGNOSIA

It would likely be challenging to get a school to formally test for prosopagnosia; even the better known cognitive issues such as dyslexia and dyscalculia are currently only inconsistently tested and addressed in a timely and effective fashion, and prosopagnosia is not nearly as well known as these are.

Assessments for both recognizing faces and comprehending emotional expression, separately administered, would be useful in understanding a child's face recognition issues, for those parents or caregivers who choose the path of formal assessment. Be aware that the number of tests currently available for children is quite limited. In fact, even the well-known Benton Facial Recognition Test, typically administered to adults, fails to consistently capture developmental prosopagnosia, according to some research (Duchaine and Wakayama 2004). In addition, just as we are beginning to comprehend the nature of prosopagnosia, whether a child can see faces normally in early childhood but experience a later onset prosopagnosia is yet to be determined. If this is possible, then early testing may not capture later problems.

One test, part of the Kaufman assessment kit (Kaufman and Kaufman 2004), offers a face recognition assessment for children ages 3–6. Although the general kit has sections on other topics for children ages 3–18, the subtest, which includes 21 questions regarding facial recognition (with fewer questions presented to the child who performs well), along with the larger kit, is usually administered by a licensed psychologist.

Assessments of a child's ability to understand facial expressions are sometimes administered by speech pathologists, child psychologists, and/or special needs educators, depending upon the school district and particular situation. Perhaps those educators who work in the area of vision, however, would also be appropriate educators for this area. Materials related to non-verbal learning disability and pragmatics, including games, worksheets, workbooks, and texts, which are available via the internet, offer practice opportunities for addressing social skills.

It would be useful to consult handbooks that deal with advocating for your child's right to testing in your specific community. Sometimes procedures related to testing protocol vary from school district to school district, and every minute of your time on this issue should be spent most effectively.

## RESEARCHERS AFFILIATED WITH UNIVERSITIES OR OTHER LABORATORIES

There can be benefits to a child's participating in university and other research because perceptive style can be revealed, if tests are effectively designed, and some research laboratories do test children. Importantly, studies may lead to greater insight into prosopagnosia, which may ultimately have an impact on lives, when that research is relevant and revealing. University testing tends to be free or can even include compensation for participation, and this can make such an option attractive for some. Sometimes testing can offer insight into perception that might not get captured in a currently available commercial test. Parents or caregivers can do an internet search for universities in their region that are involved in work on face recognition, in order to find out about testing in exchange for the child's participation in laboratory research.

It is important to keep in mind that tests can only capture what they are designed to detect—and only then if they are well designed and if principles of ethical testing are upheld. There are issues related to prosopagnosia and ways it manifests itself that may not get captured by current tests, and some prosopagnosics have reported experiencing aspects of the phenomenon that are not currently being studied. Sometimes perceptive experience does not neatly fit within a box that has been predesigned, which means that not all who are tested will come away with answers.

Remember that for years people who complained of face recognition deficit were told by doctors that their vision was "absolutely normal," and indeed, as already mentioned, even one test, the Benton, well regarded when it was first introduced, has been found in recent years to be ineffective in capturing developmental prosopagnosia.

# RIGHTS OF RESEARCH SUBJECTS WHO PARTICIPATE IN TESTING

It is important that parents be aware as to their and their children's rights with regard to research, and given the rarity of laboratory testing, it is worth mentioning these rights of parents and the responsibilities of researchers. There are protections, rules, to which professionals need adhere. As has been discussed among some prosopagnosics, there are sometimes discrepancies between points stipulated in research contracts and what actually occurs during research. These need to be reported to the Internal Review Board overseeing the laboratories if and when they occur.

If the reason for your testing is to get a written report regarding your child's face recognition ability, it is a good idea to find out ahead of time as to which laboratory results you will have access and when.

Among the rights that you and your child have, should your child participate in a study, are the following.

## Confidentiality

Every person participating in research has a right to confidentiality, if that is promised by contract. To breach confidentiality is a severe violation of professional ethics, and such behavior needs to be reported to the Internal Review Board that governs the university's or institution's laboratories. Researchers do not have a right to discuss their research subjects with those outside of the experiment without the written consent of the participant (or in the case of a child, the parent). There may be telephone numbers for the Internal Review Board on the contracts, themselves, but they can otherwise easily be found by contacting the university and asking for the Internal Review Board Department. Hang on to all contracts—which should be given before any experiments are performed. Contact the Internal Review Board of the university or institution to discuss concerns if you observe a breach of contract. Those who report violations will be helping not only their own children, but prosopagnosics in general and all who participate in laboratory experiments, by insisting that high standards in research are upheld. Along these lines, scientists working in this area should report those whom they witness violating the code of ethics to ensure that the highest standards of professionalism are enforced. Make sure to read carefully any contracts that you sign on behalf of your child, and understand her rights to confidentiality.

## Privacy and consent

Researchers need a parent's or caregiver's written permission to report or write about a child in their work or to present findings about the child.

## Professionalism

The goal of research should be to find the truth—solid, accurate, well-supported results. If the contract describes one testing scenario, that is the scenario that should occur. Laboratories cannot share your child's information without your explicit, written permission. In addition, they need to adhere to contracts. Failing to report any lack of professionalism may influence the results that get reported and slow down the field in its progress to learning the nature of prosopagnosia.

## Compensation

If compensation is promised in a written contract, it must be given. Regardless of the amount or type of compensation, the written contract is a promise to which the professional must adhere.

## Standards of accuracy

Prosopagnosics, as well as those who care about them, and the pursuit of truth in science in general, must insist upon a high level of ethics and professionalism by ensuring that scientists adhere to conduct that complies with the rules of Internal Review Boards. Scientists, like professionals in all areas, are human. You may find someone who is extremely intellectually curious, ethical, and knowledgeable, willing to work in order to glean knowledge. Skills do vary among scientists, regardless of the reputation of the specific institution for which they work, and it is important to avoid "scientist in the laboratory coat syndrome." Go into an experiment knowing what your child's rights are. A good researcher will want you to be aware of them and to understand them.

## INFORMAL FACE RECOGNITION TESTS

Please remember that an informal assessment does not have to be an actual "test," in the usual sense of the word. For most children, it is probably better to turn the activity into play, perhaps by creating a game or conversation piece, based upon the assessment itself. An informal assessment experience can actually be a growth opportunity—one of learning for the parent, who gets to understand more about the child, and one for the child, who may have quality one-on-one time with the parent.

For example, if a parent would like to learn very informally about the child's face recognition skills, she may ask her questions regarding the clothing of a familiar person in a photo—and then ask what the person's name is. Be careful—the person should not be wearing familiar clothes nor be located in a familiar context in the photo. In fact, it would be quite helpful if the hair and boundary of the face were covered, so as to avoid providing a non-facial clue. If the child does not recognize the familiar person, this should be taken in stride (e.g. it would not necessarily help the child to exclaim, "Oh, my gosh! You don't even know that is Ricardo? But you play with him every day!") Learn what and how the child recognizes, what she sees, and then use that information to help her to navigate the social world. The point here is not to be "secretive" per se, but rather to let the child feel comfortable with being the person that she was born to be.

The following test ideas, informally applied, may provide some insight into a child's face recognition skills. They can be used by parents or professionals; however, a teacher who wishes to perform an assessment should probably discuss this with the parent ahead of time. At the very least, she should consult whatever rules are in place in her district regarding these issues. Results cannot be considered to be conclusive when tests are administered informally, because they are not scientific in nature. However, informal tests can be extremely revealing for a parent or professional attempting to gain insight into a child's needs. At times, informal testing can even lead to greater insight than that offered via formal testing, and should therefore always be considered.

## ONLINE WEBSITES AND INTERNET SEARCHES

Online websites, easy to find using keywords such as "face recognition tests," can be useful. Please be aware that most of these assessments, at the time of writing in 2009, are generally scored for adults, rather than children. It is possible that differences in face recognition could influence the "normalcy" of these tests, given variations in age range. In addition, such issues as children's test-taking skills, or even exposure to famous faces based on age, could influence scores.[2] Distractions for the child tested online at home, speed of

---

2   Please note that one or more studies (e.g., Anastasa and Rhodes 2005) have suggested an "own age bias" in face recognition, which could influence test scores. That is, the research states that children and older adults have been found to test better on recognition tests that involve viewing faces of their own age.

computer, and help from others while test taking can also affect test results. Therefore, some level of caution is warranted when using these online face tests and interpreting results when working with children.

### Online virtual hair salons

These provide opportunity to see how familiar people would look by wearing a different hairstyle. The user can upload photos of those known to the child. With permission, take photos ofChange the hairstyle and print. Include these photos, along with others (unfamiliar faces) to determine whether the child can identify the familiar person with the different hairstyle and/or color.

Word of caution: some prosopagnosics can use facial expression to recognize, and it could be wise to include photos that have as close to neutral facial expressions as possible. In addition, make sure that the person in the photo is not wearing clothing familiar to the prosopagnosic. Context should also be neutral (that is, a simple white or colored background, rather than the living room of someone's home).

### Online virtual hair salons with photos of famous people

Some online hair salons have photos of famous people and enable the user to change the hairstyle and clothing that the famous person is wearing. You can try a similar informal check for face recognition to that above by changing the hairstyle and clothes to see whether your child still recognizes the person's face.

### Changing features in photos

A simple test would be to white-out the hair and clothes of a Xerox color copy of familiar people. A school webpage, for example, may provide photos of those whom the child is likely to know. In addition, your computer's paint technology may enable you to "erase" the person's hair and other clues.

Use a digital camera and touch-up program to test for recognition of familiar faces. With permission, take photos of people that your child knows well. Change non-facial aspects of the photo (hair, clothing, etc.). For those who lack a computer photo program for altering photos (cropping, etc.), it might be possible to ask a friend or check at the school or local library to gain access to such a camera and program. They are fairly commonly used.

Take pictures of familiar people wearing hats, sunglasses, and unfamiliar clothes in unfamiliar contexts. Be careful, however. If the child knows that you took the photo or is aware of the places in the photo, she may guess who the people are by using those clues.

Be mindful when testing not to give context clues. You might even want to include some photos of people that you don't know.

Informal tests such as the facial expression recognition test found in the Appendix of *Emotions Revealed* by Paul Ekman (2003) may also be useful, even if not by any means conclusive, under informal circumstances. There are also online tests mentioned earlier. Although these are generally normed for adults, it is hoped that reliable online tests for children will become available, free of charge, in the near future.

# Chapter 14

# LOOKING TOWARD THE FUTURE

Thus far, we have discussed what prosopagnosia is, some ideas for how face recognition deficit may have an impact on the life of a child and his development, and examined specific suggestions for addressing prosopagnosia at home and in the community. These ideas, which will need to be revised according to the needs of the specific child and his supporters, are offered as the start of a conversation about prosopagnosia and childhood. They will also need to be changed and/or broadened as more comes to be known about prosopagnosia and childhood.

There is a great deal to be learned about prosopagnosia in the future, as research into perceptive style deepens, technology enhances the potential to meet learner needs, and educators, visual rehabilitation specialists, and speech therapists communicate more effectively with scientists, neurologists, and psychologists to support those with face recognition deficit.

The question of predicting who will develop atypical face processing is an interesting and relevant one. As earlier discussed, there is evidence of a genetic predisposition, and also those infants who have cataract surgeries even during the first months of life appear likely to develop prosopagnosia, some of the research suggests (Le Grand *et al.* 2004). Can this lack of access to facial information during a critical visual learning period influence an outcome of atypical face processing? Some have discussed informally on the internet the question of those children who are born with extremely blurred vision and develop prosopagnosia. Could the issue of visual acuity, when it has an impact on full access to faces in infancy, influence the development of face recognition deficit? And for those born prematurely, where initial visual exposure may be atypical or occur during an atypical period of development, are there issues related to face recognition that need be explored? Indeed, whether a post-birth event may be the cause of prosopagnosia, even among children who appear to have a genetic predisposition (that is, they have prosopagnosic relatives) is a question worthy of further research. Only time and earnest study will tell. And this is crucial, since, if it is the case that lack of visual opportunity prevents the development of face recognition, perhaps it will also be true that exposure to specific visual opportunities (or even medication) early on, for these populations, will prevent or remediate the issue. Such remedies would only be recommended for children, given the difficulty with adaptation to new senses and perceptive opportunities that adults face, according to research into the areas of vision and cochlear implants (Gregory and Wallace 1963; Mindick 2005b).

Furthermore, if impairment in facial processing is an expectable outcome for children who undergo cataract surgeries in infancy, as a paper by Le Grand *et al.* suggests (2004), then optometrists, ophthalmologists, and, importantly, parents of the children concerned, ought to be educated as to this fact. This should, in turn, lead the research toward addressing early intervention issues. It would be useful to offer ideas regarding support to those parents in terms of the prosopagnosia, in case it does occur. Simply put, it is imperative that, if prosopagnosia is an expectable outcome in some circumstances, we act as effectively as possible toward providing support and educating those for whom it is expected.

These issues are important not only in western nations, in which even early surgical interventions for cataract removal for infants can result in cognitive visual deficit due to missed critical learning periods, but also in such developing nations as India and Nepal, where preventable blindness is rampant, volunteer organizations commonly provide post-infancy surgeries, including cataract surgeries, there is very little medical or psychosocial follow-up, and, importantly, failure of treatment (and failure to recognize what one sees may be considered a lack of cure) may have certain religious implications, viewed as religious punishment by the community. In cases of public policy in developing nations, for example, understanding the impact of lost critical visual learning opportunities could guide government funding decisions to target funds to reach infants more rapidly.

Given that the old assumption that "everyone can recognize faces" is not true, this could mean that employers in specific professions that rely heavily on face recognition might benefit from conducting face recognition tests. As even highly intelligent people can fail miserably at what for many is considered to be a simple social skill, where national security is at issue, for example, face recognition should not be assumed. This should not prevent the individual from working in national security or from gaining excellent positions professionally (indeed, anecdotally, there are prosopagnosics at various institutions of higher learning who do succeed well), but rather, it should help the individual to more appropriately find his talent niche.

In addition, there are cases that have been widely reported in which survivors of crimes have made significant identity errors resulting in individuals' being wrongfully convicted, sometimes imprisoned for years, based on the incorrect eyewitness testimony that included facial identity errors. In the case described in *Picking Cotton* (Cannino, Cotton, and Torneo 2009), for example, a man was put in solitary and was on death row for a crime which DNA evidence proved years later he did not commit. Of course, one does not need to be prosopagnosic in order to make an identity error. This having been said, an important question needs to be addressed: should courtroom cases, which rely solely on facial identification as a means for determining guilt, require facial recognition testing? Our growing understanding of the prevalence of prosopagnosia requires that we at least explore this possibility. Given the fact that many in the general population are unaware that they have face recognition deficit, it stands to reason that there may be some whose ability is far inferior to that of the general population. Should police officers, security guards, and airport personnel have to take facial recognition tests?

It is also important to look at the question of rebound. Those who were born with recognition ability, have acquired prosopagnosia as adults, and regain their ability to recognize faces tend to be happy with that opportunity and do not appear to suffer an adjustment period with regard to that rebound. There are, indeed, documented and anecdotal cases of recovery from prosopangosia—for example, one when prosopagnosia was acquired by stroke and the individual regained ability to recognize faces, as the Hier, Mondlock, and Caplan (1983) study showed. Importantly, the research into adult acquired prosopagnosia should begin to probe those cases of rebound, the return to face sight, for example, because this could be useful for stroke victims. Only by more closely studying these cases will we become better able to predict who will rebound, and better able to help those who acquire face recognition deficit as adults. Perhaps there are strategies, which those rebounding individuals unknowingly use, and which contribute to their success. On the other hand, as studies (Bower 2003; Gregory and Wallace 1963; Von Sendon 1960) into the recovery of sight by individuals who have been blind from childhood suggest, for those who are born with blindness (or go blind in childhood) and are blind long term, we know that gaining new, unaccustomed visual ability can be traumatic.

Increasingly, devices are being invented and/or marketed to offer improved face recognition technology. For example, "Memory Glasses" from

MIT's Media Laboratory can recognize previously input faces and tell the viewer orally or in print message the name of the person within viewing range of the device. Significant progress has been made in the past decade, and this is likely to continue. Indeed, there may be ways in which to combine camera technologies to take some of the guessing out of daily living for the prosopagnosic child. Given the rapid changes in technology that are occurring, it appears that, as previously mentioned, one of the most useful skills that an educator can offer a prosopagnosic is the ability to learn to identify relevant technology itself, and inventively strive to adapt it to their recognition needs.

In addition, research into those who have been successful with learning recognition techniques should take place and longitudinal studies undertaken to determine whether those programs currently being used—for example, those related to emociagnosia—should incorporate some of these strategies. The question of whether the countless hours and funds spent toward educating people to recognize emotional expressions (e.g. in speech therapy) have meaningful impact needs to be examined.

In terms of past experiments, if it is true that two percent of the population is prosopagnosic, then it is likely that experiments already done which relate to face recognition may have been normed by prosopagnosics, along with non-prosopagnosic individuals, because some of these were normed at a time when face recognition deficit was considered rare.

And there are other issues. It usually takes time for us as children then becoming adolescents and finally adults to learn to empathize, to step into other people's shoes, to deeply comprehend how our actions have an impact on those about whom we care or with whom we are simply acquainted— even for those for whom perceiving emotional expressions is not difficult. For a prosopagnosic, it can take real work, social insight, and careful, apt reflection and time, to which one may lack access, to eventually come to understand the ins-and-outs of the social realm while minimizing the number of "pickles" into which one gets oneself. Those reading this who have face recognition impairment may understand exactly what this means. For example, it can mean introducing oneself to one's aunt or cousin at a family gathering. Or congratulating the wrong person on an award that has just been won. It can influence professional interactions. For those challenged with regard to recognizing emotional expressions, having trouble when finding that people are angry or annoyed, apparently out of the blue, can be fairly daunting.

In addition, if it takes until one's adult years for some prosopagnosic individuals to identify their own facial recognition challenges, then one can imagine how difficult it is for the average non-prosopagnosic to understand what prosopagnosia is and to refrain from taking offense at recognition mistakes.

That snobby neighbor who never says hello when you see him in the grocery store may (or may not) have a recognition problem. That friend who is usually very kind, but who bores everyone by talking incessantly, may lack access to the social cues and could benefit from more blunt—but sensitive, well-timed, and helpful—feedback. What if these individuals had been reached in childhood, instead of in their adult years? Or not at all?

I am hoping, striving, for a world in which these issues are better understood, with regard to prosopagnosia and beyond. This is important because, as good neighbors, we should learn to live together, and to reach across difference, while demanding the thoughtful consideration of others.

While the first several thousand years of human history have arguably been spent in determining as to what our commonalities are as human beings, it can be argued that the past two decades have been used exploring and discovering our great diversity—and that includes cognitive diversity—as a species. The varied ways in which humans perceive provide opportunity for accomplishments, for talents, that may well be beyond our imagination. Tapping this talent and learning to thrive as a society in a manner that enables us to communicate across perceptive difference is an important goal. We need to look at ourselves and each other with frankness and clarity and to start—or in some cases, maintain—the conversation. This is utterly crucial to our bolstering human intellect, creativity, art, potential. But first we have to recognize the challenge.

# AFTERWORD

Prosopagnosia is "cognitive home" for me. While some may complain, I learned some time ago that regardless of the problems that I have as a prosopagnosic, there are also benefits, the most important of which is that it is who I am. Like the paintings that decorate the walls of a house or even its furniture, my memories influence what I know, how I see, whom and how I remember, who I am. I'm okay with that.

How to handle who one is with grace can be challenging at times. But once I know your name, I will remember your stories. There's a cabin in a wood shared with classmates or a green field where you run, a ball flying. The shared stories of our lives become the very fabric of my world, a thread of emotion stitched across my days. Emotion is my world. I am a prosopagnosic who can see emotional expressions, and people's stories are what I remember.

Other prosopagnosics may instead be strong in math and navigation, and able to spend hours with numbers in their heads, open a map in their minds, know a city with eyes shut, just by remembering an atlas that they had looked at, perhaps only a few times. These straight and curved lines form patterns that enable these prosopagnosics to follow various kinds of passion, to build walls and machines of numbers, to expand and broaden our shared world in different ways.

I do not know when I first became prosopagnosic, but my first memory of a major non-recognition incident came during my teenage years. However, I suspect that my prosopagnosia is developmental in nature, because a close relative has had a face recognition deficit since childhood. It was not until I was well into adulthood that I began investigating face recognition deficit. Whether prosopagnosia can be developmental but not manifest until the teenage years is a question for future research, although it is possible that

I, like many, simply did not notice issues related to face recognition until those differences became truly problematic in adulthood.

So it's about learning. And learning is like going down a long, fun, exciting slope in a toboggan at night, steering safely to the trip's end. In the meantime, the universe passes in a glimpse, and cold stars wink under snow. The world, in shades of black and gray, reveals itself.

The great thing about talking is the possible fluidity of a conversation, but books are solids. Socrates warned of the danger of books, was afraid of freezing a monologue in time and space. But my hope is to create change. I don't want this book to be a solid. I hope that you will carry part of it away with you, change it, challenge it, argue or agree. I am hoping for a fluid book—one that will contribute to change while reflecting it.

# APPENDIX

## THEORIES OF DEVELOPMENT

In Chapter 4, I described the pattern perception that I believe influences the perception of faces, math, and navigation, an ability which I would suggest frames human understanding.

Now I would like to explain as to how I believe that this understanding evolves.

Given the fact that a child is able to see the distance to her mother's eyes while nursing, combined with the limited visual acuity that the infant has, it makes sense that she would be visually attracted to the brightness and darkness of the pupils. As the ability to frame the motional patterns that exist in the world evolves, the infant ultimately confronts a significant sensory challenge: that of comprehending a moving face, sorting through the motions of eyes, cheeks, head, neck, etc. in order to comprehend the face.

Think of it this way: if it were not for the infant's having a way in which to cognitively draw a line through space, an invisible line across the eyes to serve as a reference point, how could she ever keep track of all of the motions that the challenge of comprehending the face presents? Eventually, as described in Chapter 4, I believe that this comprehension—that is, this ability to set two points in space and navigate around motional patterns—will influence the further ability to understand far more than this.

What we see and perceive becomes the world around us; this, in turn, becomes our internal culture, the world within us. The same is true of perception across every sense.

And both of these worlds—the external and internal, mentally represented world—require a comprehension of motion, for motion is, in a word, change. Understanding any change on earth, whether melody of a song, the colors that blend across the picture on an artist's easel, the changing sounds that form the words that fall from our lips, requires the perception of motion. In a sense, one might consider the human mind—indeed, the thinking of all species—to possess a different kind of relativity: the relative perception of motion, which has an impact on cognition. We need a language for discussing the interactive worlds of the physically perceived and the mentally represented. Here is a proposal:

Intra: Refers to the world of mentally represented sensory perceptions

Extra: Refers to our sensory organs' physically perceiving the world, the world of externally represented symbols that the individual perceives with the senses

Intra-extra or combi: Refers to the two combined, when recognition occurs.

Therefore, we can describe the visual mental representation by using the term "intravisual," the tactile mental representation with intratactile, intra-aural, etc. The physical act of seeing (the sensory interaction which takes place when the eye and brain together process an external, visual image) would be extra-visual, the act of physically touching would be extratactile, extra-aural, etc. This pertains to every sense.

The act of mentally representing a visual image would be intravisual; a tactile image would be intratactile, intra-aural, etc. as pertains to every sense.

The act of recognition would be combivisual, combitactile, combi-aural, etc.

Just as we build towers around us, we also build towers within us—the mentally represented sensory images that become our external and internal worlds. As humans, we adapt not only to the world around us, but also to the world within us, the world of mental representations.

It can be argued that every intelligence style has its notation. It was very interesting to do a limited study (Mindick 2005b) with some remarkable people (and in some cases, the families of those people) who had gained the senses of either sight or sound following long-term deprivation of the respective senses. The aim of the study was to begin to find out about how we learn to recognize, and to discover how people adapt to new senses when they have to learn those senses for the first time. Those who have had sight-enabling surgeries or cochlear implants following long-term sensory deprivation face a major challenge, perhaps the greatest challenge that one could have. It is fairly rare in adult life to have to learn a sense or to perceive an entirely new experience. The individuals with whom I spoke found that they needed to learn the sense from scratch. This is no small feat when one considers that mastering a sense is a bit like mastering a language, and one needs to gain fluency in the sense. They needed to learn what I would like to call the notation of those senses.

That is, in order for a child who has been born mostly deaf prior to surgery for cochlear implant to comprehend that the sound of water that he hears is a bathtub nearly full, he must be able to recognize first the sound of water. He must also know that when liquid falls into a partly filled container, the sound of water falling will be of an increasingly lower pitch. Similarly, in order for an individual who has been long-term deprived of vision to comprehend that a drawing on a sheet of paper is of a table, he needs to first understand that the lines which are the visual edges of objects usually look dark, in comparison with the rest of the object. Every sense and learning style has its basic, elemental notation, the fundamental blocks which, when effectively perceived, enable us to form mental representations of those symbols. A person newly hearing (who has been deaf for years) who begins to be able to discriminate the sounds of various kinds of "beeps" from a cochlear implant may eventually gain enough fluency to recognize the sound of a doorbell, for example. The mastery of recognition ability appeared to follow a language paradigm. That is, individuals needed to gain fluency in the sense.

In *Resolution theory*, which I began writing in 2002 and continued to work on until 2005, as well as in other papers, I describe in greater detail my theories related to these topics. However, for now, suffice to say:

Like the phonemes that comprise language, each sense has its basic, elemental notation that needs to be perceived, mentally represented, interacted with, and built. Motional perception influences access to sensory notation; this, in turn, influences what gets mentally represented, intrasensed, which then influences how mental representations interact and develop. The individual's ability to biocognitively perceive with accuracy various kinds of notation will influence which aspects of our intellect have the opportunity to develop. Let me be clear: the individual's ability to perceive motion—and the kinds of patterns to which this gives her access, combined with other issues, such as physical availability of the organs of sense—will ultimately determine the development of her learning style. This process of the evolution of learning style, as determined by access to sensory notation, which is determined by (among other things) the ability to perceive motion, can be called Intellectiogenesis. Here's what I'm saying:

- Math is not an intelligence style on its own. Pattern perception, including, for example, faces, math, and navigation, is.

- There is an interaction between individual and environment that will enable an individual to build cognitive towers of understanding in a process that I call Intellectiogenesis. Notational access is needed for this to occur.

## IMPLICATIONS FOR EDUCATION

When an individual has limited access to a particular notational system, whether that is one related to facial expression that could lead to social understanding or math notation that could lead to comprehension of how patterns of numbers get organized, then she needs to be offered information in alternative ways that enable her to circumvent the requirement. In terms of emotional expression, this can mean offering verbally the information to which she lacks visual or aural access. I have tried to offer in this book ideas for alternatives to the notation of social understanding, so that information can be provided to the individual (in most cases) discreetly and also effectively. In terms of math notation, an individual who lacks access to Arabic numerals should be offered symbol systems which she can access. Our technology makes this possible, and the idea of altering notational systems (in a manner similar to that which Braille accomplishes for the blind) should be further explored.

These questions are relevant, in that all learning is, in essence, an act of recognition. While it can be argued that in the past individuals needed to adapt their needs to match opportunities afforded by technology, the opportunity exists today for finding ways in which to adapt notation to fit the individual. In terms of social understanding, whether simply offering verbal information for one who lacks access to the language of facial expression is a question that some have pursued. It is also worth pursuing offering alternative access via technology in more inventive ways, as some laboratories are already accomplishing.

There needs to be a discipline specifically for recognition studies that is devoted to the questions of how we recognize, how we learn to recognize, and how this can inform strategies for individualizing learning.

# GLOSSARY

**Biocognitively**: This refers to the interaction that occurs when the physical, external world is biologically perceived and cognitively grasped. Biological and cognitive combined.

**Emociagnosia**: Inability to see and comprehend emotional facial expression. In some cases, this may be accompanied by lack of perceptive access to vocal prosody to communicate emotion.

**Emocioperception**: This term is used to describe the perception, the comprehension, of another's emotional experience, usually as communicated via facial expression or vocal prosody (vocal intonation). It can also be experienced if one notes another's gestures, for example, or by tactile means if, for example, one comprehends another's emotional experience by understanding that the tightening of a grip on one's hand means that the person is experiencing worry. (To be clear, this is to say that even a person both blind and deaf would, of course, be able to have emocioperceptive ability.)

**Genderization**: The act of slanting questions or discoveries in such a way in research as to cause a narrow (to the point of inaccurate) understanding of how a phenomenon has an impact on people of one or the other gender.

**Intellectiogensis**: The development of learning style in accordance with that individual's perceptive access to the notation of that learning style, as influenced by her relative perception of the world's motions.

**Maladapt**: To adapt to a challenge in a manner that is either ineffective or less effective than some of the other available coping strategies. To adapt in a manner that unnecessarily limits the individual.

**Neurotypical**: In this book, the term refers to people who are not prosopagnosic.

**Non-prosopagnosic**: This is a person who has normal or superior ability to recognize faces.

**Normally sighted**: Although this may have many meanings in varied contexts, in this book it means, "non-prosopagnosic."

**Photomotion**: The perception of math, topography, and faces, which are inextricably linked through what I assert is a single pattern perception ability that humans possess.

# BIBLIOGRAPHY

## INTRODUCTION

Autism Speaks™ (2007) *The 8th Annual International Meeting for Autism Research*. Available at www.autismspeaks.org/science/science_news/imfar_2009_day_three. php, accessed on 24 May 2010.

Dworzynski, K., Happe, F. and Ronald, A. (2009) 'Gender effects in autism spectrum disorders: symptom and intelligence differences in a population-based twin study.' Poster presented at International Meeting for Autism Research, May 2009. Available at www.imfor.confex.com/imfor/2009/webprogram/Paper4799.ht, accessed on 18 March 2010 .

Grüter, M., Grüter, T., Bell, V., Horst, J., *et al.* (2007) 'Hereditary prosopagnosia: the first case series.' *Cortex 43*, 734–749.

Kennerknecht, I., Grüter, M., Grüter, T., Otte, S., Neumann, T. *et al.* (2002) *First Report on the Genetics of Prospagnosia*. Strassborg, France: Poster European Congress of Human Genetics, 10, 1.

Kennerknecht, I., Grüter, T., Welling, B., Wentzek, S. *et al.* (2006) 'First report on the genetics of prosopagnosia (HPA).' *European Journal of Human Genetics 10*, (xxx 1), 249.

Nakayama, K., Garrido, L., Russell, R., Chabris, C.F., Gerbasi, M. and Duchaine, B.C. (2006) 'Developmental prosopagnosia: phenotypes and estimated prevalence.' *Society for Neuroscience Abstracts*, No. 702.9.

Von Baker, M. (2010) 'The overlooked autism of girls, and what comes after'. *The Sunbreak News*. Available at www.thesunbreak.com/the-overlooked-autism-of-girls-and-what-comes-after, accessed on 25 March 2010.

## CHAPTER 1

Alperin, G. (n.d.) *Prosopagnosia: An Introduction to and FAQ about a Most Peculiar Condition*. Available at http://home.earthlink.net/~blankface/prosopagnosia.shtml, accessed on 24 May 2010.

Avidan, G. and Behrmann, M. (2008) 'Implicit familiarity processing in congenital prosopagnosia.' *Journal of Neuropsychology 2*, 141–164.

Behrmann, M., Avidan, G., Marotta, J. and Kimchi, R. (2005) 'Detailed exploration of face-related processing in congenital prosopagnosia: 1. Behavioral findings.' *Journal of Cognitive Neuroscience 17*, 7, 1130–1149.

Burman, C. (n.d.) *Welcome to my Pages about Prosopagnosia*. Available at www.prosopagnosia.com/, accessed on 24 May 2010.

Busigny, T., Joubert, S., Felician, O. and Rossion, B. (2008) 'Processing upright and inverted faces in acquired prosopagnosic patients with no object recognition deficits [Abstract].' *Journal of Vision 8*, 6, 156–156a. Available at www.journalofvision.org/content/8/6/156, accessed on 25 May 2010.

Choisser, B. (1997) *Face Blind!* Available at www.choisser.com/faceblind, accessed on 25 May 2010.

Darwin, C. (1998) *The Expression of Emotion in Man and Animals*. New York: Oxford University Press.

Duchaine, B., Parker, H. and Nakayama, K. (2003) 'Normal recognition of emotion in a prosopagnosic.' *Perception 32*, 827–838.

Farah, M., Wilson, K., Drain, M. and Tanaka, J. (1995) 'The inverted face inversion effect in prosopagnosia: evidence for mandatory, face-specific perceptual mechanisms.' *Vision Research 35*, 14, 2089–2093.

Gardner, H. (1993) *Multiple Intelligences: The Theory in Practice*. New York: Basic Books.

Grueter, M., Grueter, T., Bell, V., Horst, J. *et al.* (2007) 'Hereditary prosopagnosia: the first case series.' *Cortex 43*, 734–749.

Humphreys, K., Avidan, G. and Behrmann, M. (2007) 'A detailed investigation of facial expression processing in congenital prosopagnosia as compared to acquired prosopagnosia.' *Experimental Brain Research 176*, 2, 356–373.

Laskowski, W. (1999) *Suddenly I No Longer Recognized Faces*. Available at www.choisser.com/faceblind/wolfgang.html, accessed on 7 April 2009.

Le Grand, R., Mondloch, C., Maurer, D. and Brent, H. (2004) 'Impairment in holistic face processing following early visual deprivation.' *Le Psychological Science 15*, ,11, 762–768.

Peelen, M.V., Lucas, N., Mayer, E. and Vuilleumier, P. (2009) 'Emotional attention in acquired prosopagnosia.' *Social Cognitive and Affective Neuroscience 4*, 43, 268–277.

Russell, R., Duchaine, B. and Nakayama, K. (2009) 'Brief reports super-recognizers: people with extraordinary face recognition ability.' *Psychonomic Bulletin & Review 16*, 2, 252–257.

Zhu, Q., Song, Y., Hu, S. and Li, X. (2009) 'Heritability of the specific cognitive ability of face perception.' *Current Biology 20*, 2, 137–142.

# CHAPTER 2

Anderson, J.R. (1984) 'The development of self-recognition: a review.' *Developmental Psychobiology 17*, 1, 35–49.

Anisfeld, E. (1982) 'The onset of social smiling in preterm and full-term infants from two ethnic backgrounds.' *Infant Behavior and Development 5*, 2–4, 387–395.

Aslin, D. (1993) 'Infant Accommodation and Convergence.' In K. Simons (ed.) *Early Visual Development Normal and Abnormal.* New York: Oxford University Press.

Barrera, M. and Mauer, D. (1981) 'The perception of facial expressions by the three-month-old.' *Child Development 5*, 203–206.

Bertenthal, B. and Fischer, K. (1978) 'Development of self-recognition in the infant.' *Developmental Psychology 14*, 1, 44–50.

Braddick, O., Atkinson, J., French, J. and Howland, HC. (1979) 'Photorefractive study of infant accommodation.' *Vision Research 19*, 1319–1330.

Brookman, K. (ed.) (1983) 'Ocular accommodation in human infants.' *American Journal of Optometry and Physiological Optics 60*, 91–99.

Brown, A. and Lindsey, D. (2009) 'Contrast insensitivity: the critical immaturity in infant visual performance.' *Optometry and Vision Science 86*, 6, 572–576.

Bushnell, I. (2001) 'Mother's face recognition in newborn infants: learning and memory.' *Infant and Child Development 10*, 67–74.

Cohen, L. and Cashon, C. (2001) 'Do 7-month-old infants process independent features or facial configurations?' *Infant and Child Development 10*, 83–92.

Darwin, C. (1987) *The Expression of Emotion in Man and Animals.* New York: Oxford University Press.

Ekman, P. (2003) *Emotions Revealed.* New York: Times Books.

Fagan, J.F. (1972) 'Infants' recognition memory for faces.' *Journal of Experimental Psychology 14*, 453–476.

Fine, I., Wade, A., Brewer, A.A., May, M.G., Boynton, G.M., Wandell, B.A. *et al.* 'The effects of long-term deprivation on visual perception and visual cortex.' *Nature Neuroscience 6*, 915–991.

Gagnon, M., Gosselin, P., Hudon-ver der Buhs, I., larocque, K. and Millard, K. (2010) 'Children's recognition and discrimination of fear and disgust facial expression.' *Journal of Nonverbal Behaviour 34*, 27–42.

Gauthier, I. and Nelson, C.A. (2001) 'The development of face expertise.' *Current Opinion in Neurobiology. Special Issue: Cognitive Neuroscience 11*, 219–224.

Goren, C.C., Sarty, M. and Wu, P.Y. (1975) 'Visual following and pattern discrimination of face-like stimuli by newborn infants.' *Pediatrics 56*, 4, 544–549.

Gregory, R. and Wallace, J. (1963) *Recovery from Early Blindness: A Case Study.* Available at www.richardgregory.org/papers/recovery_blind/recovery-from-early-blindness.pdf, accessed on 8 February 2005.

Haynes, H., White, B.L. and Held, R. (1965) 'Visual accommodation in human infants.' *Science 148*, 3669, 528–530.

Johnson, S., Slaughter, V. and Carey, S. (2000) 'Whose gaze will infants follow? The elicitation of gaze following in 12-month-olds.' *Developmental Science 12*, 233–238.

Kahana-Kalman, R. and Walker-Andrews, A. (2001) 'The role of person familiarity in young infants' perception of emotional expressions.' *Child Development 72*, 2, 352–369.

Karmiloff, K. and Karmiloff-Smith, A. (1998) *Everything Your Baby Would Ask…If Only Babies Could Talk*. Buffalo, NY: Firefly Books.

Kaufmann, F. (1995) 'The development of motion perception in early infancy.' *European Journal of Pediatrics 154*, Supplement 4, April.

Kennerknecht, I., Grueter, T., Welling, B., Wentzek, S. *et al.* (2006) 'First report of prevalence of non-syndromic hereditary prosopagnosia (HPA).' *American Journal of Medical Genetics Part A 140A*, 1617–1622.

Kuchuk, A., Vibbert, M. and Bornstein, M. (1986) 'The perception of smiling and its experiential correlates in 3-month-old infants.' *Child Development 57*, 1054–1061.

Le Grand, R., Mondloch, C.J., Maurer, D. and Brent, H.P. (2004) 'Impairment in holistic face processing following early visual deprivation.' *Psychological Science 15*, 11, 762–768.

Ludemann, P. and Nelson, C.A. (1988) 'The categorical representation of facial expressions by 7-month-old infants.' *Developmental Psychology 24*, 492–501.

Maurer, D. and Lewis, T.L. (2001) 'Visual acuity: the role of visual input in inducing postnatal change.' *Clinical Neuroscience Research 1*, 239–247.

Mindick, N. (2005b) 'Adaptation to new senses.' unpublished manuscript (presented at Harvard Graduate School of Education Conference, January.

Mondloch, C.J., Dobson, K.S., Parson, J. and Maurer, D. *et al.* (2004) 'Why 8-year-olds can't tell the difference between Steve Martin and Paul Newman: factors contributing to the slow development of sensitivity to the spacing of facial features.' *Journal of Experimental Child Psychology 89*, 159–181.

Mondloch, C.J., Lewis, T.L., Budreau, D.R., Maurer, D. *et al.* (1999) 'Face perception during early infancy.' *Psychological Science 10*, 419–422.

Mondloch, C.J., Maurer, D. and Ahola, S. (2006) 'Becoming a face expert.' *Psychological Science 17*, 930–934.

Nelson, C. (1987) 'The recognition of facial expressions in the first two years of life mechanisms of development.' *Child Development 57*, 4, 1054–1061.

Nelson, C. (2001) 'The development and neural bases of face recognition.' *Infant and Child Development 10*, 1–2, 3–18.

Otsuka, Y., Nakato, E., Kanazawa, S., Masami, K. *et al.* (2007) 'Neural activation to upright and inverted faces in infants measured by near infrared spectroscopy.' *NeuroImage 34*, 1, 399–406.

Pascalis, O. and de Schonen S. (1994) 'Recognition memory in 3- to 4-day-old human neonates.' *Neuroreport 5*, 14, 1721–1724.

Pascalis, O., de Haan, M. and Nelson, C. (2002) 'Is face processing species-specific during the first year of life?' *Science 296*, 5561, 1321–1323.

Pascalis, O., de Schonen, S., Morton, J., Deruelle, C. and Fabre-Grenet, M. (1995) 'Mother's face recognition by neonates: a replication and an extension.' *Infant Behavior and Development 18*, 79–85.

Patterson, M.L. and Werker, J.F. (2002) 'Infants ability to match dynamic phonetic and gender information in the face and voice'. *Journal of Experimental Child Psychology, 81*, 1 93–115.

Piaget, J. (1977) *The Essential Piaget: An Interpretive Reference and Guide*. Gruber, H.E. and Vonèche, J.J. (eds). New York: Basic Books.

Rose, S.A., Jankowski, J.J., Feldman, J.F. (2008) 'The inversion effect in infancy: the role of internal and external features', 3, 470–480.

Rosenblum, L.D., Yakel, D.A., Baseer, N., Panchal, A., Nordarse, B.C. and Niehus, R.P. (2002) 'Visual speech information for face recognition.' *Perception and Psychophysics 64*, 2, 220–229.

Tanaka, J.W. and Farah, M.J. (1993) 'Parts and wholes in face recognition'. *Quarterly Journal of Experimental Psychology, 46A*, 225–245.

Turati, C. Sangrigoli, S. Ruel, J. de Schonen, S. (2004) Evidence of the Fave Inversion Effect in 4-Month-Old Infants. *Infancy, 6*, 2, 275–297.

Serrano, J.M., Iglesias, J. and Loeches, A. (1992) 'Visual discrimination and recognition of facial expressions of anger, fear, and surprise in 4-to-6-month-old infants.' *Developmental Psychobiology 25*, 411–425.

Soken, N.H. and Pick, A.D. (1992) 'Intermodal perception of happy and angry expressive behaviors by seven-month-old infants.' *Child Development 63*, 787–795.

Spitz, R.A. (1965) *The First Year of Life: A Psychoanalytic Study of Normal and Deviant Development of Object Relations*. New York: International Universities Press.

Stucki, M., Kaufmann-Hayoz, R. and Kaufmann, F. (1987) 'Infants' recognition of a face revealed through motion: contribution of internal facial movement and head movement.' *Journal of Experimental Psychology 44*, 180–91.

Suttle, C., Banks, M. and Graf, E. (2002) 'FPL and sweep VEP to tritan stimuli in young human infants.' *Vision Research 42*, 26, 2879–2891.

Schwarzer, G., Zauner, N. and Jovanovic, B. (2007) 'Evidence of a shift from featural to configural face processing in infancy'. *Developmental Science, 10*, 452–463.

Young-Brown, G., Rosenfeld, H.M. and Horowitz, F.D. (1977) 'Infant discrimination of facial expressions.' *Child Development 49*, 555–562.

# CHAPTER 3

Baby Milestones. 'Parenting The home of Parenting and Babytalk'. Available at www.parenting.com/article/Baby/Development/parenting-guide-baby-milestmer. Accessed on 27 June 2010.

Connolly, M. (2010) 'Your baby: ten milestones for the first two years.' CNN.com Health Parenting. Available at www.cnn.com/2007/HEALTH/parenting/06/07/par.baby.milestones/index.html. Accessed on 27 June 2010.

Maslow, A.H. (1943) 'A theory of human motivation.' *Psychological Review 50*, 370–396. Available at http://psychclassics.yorku.ca/Maslow/motivation.htm, accessed on 27 May 2010.


# CHAPTER 4

Alperin, G. (n.d.) *Prosopagnosia: An Introduction to and FAQ about a Most Peculiar Condition.* Available at www.home.earthlink.net/~blankface/prosopagnosia.shtml, accessed on 24 May 2010.

Baron-Cohen, S., Spitz, A. and Cross, P. (1993) 'Do children with autism recognise surprise? A research note.' *Cognition and Emotion 7*, 6, 507–516.

Begeer, S. (2006) 'Attention to facial emotion expressions in children with autism.' *Autism 10*, 1, 37–51.

Burman, C. (n.d.) *Welcome to my Pages about Prosopagnosia.* Available at www.prosopagnosia.com/, accessed on 24 May 2010.

Choisser, B. (1997) *Face Blind!* Available at www.choisser.com/faceblind, accessed on 25 May 2010.

Devlin, K. (2001) *The Math Gene: How Mathematical Thinking Evolved and Why Numbers are Like Gossip.* New York: Basic Books.

Ellemberg, D., Lewis, T., Defina, N., Maurer, D. *et al.* (2005) 'Greater losses in sensitivity to second-order local motion than to first-order local motion after early visual deprivation in humans.' *Vision Research 45*, 2877–2884.

Freitag, C.M, Konrad, C., Häberlen, M., Kleser, C. *et al.* (2008) 'Perception of biological motion in autism spectrum disorders.' *Neuropsychologia 46*, 5, 1480–1494.

Grandin, T. (2006) *Thinking In Pictures, Expanded Edition: My Life with Autism.* New York: Vintage Books.

Klin, A., Sparrow, S., de Bildt, A., Cicchetti, D.V. *et al.* (1999) 'A normed study of face recognition in autism and related disorders.' *Journal of Autism and Developmental Disorders 29*, 6, 499–508.

Milne, E., White, S., Campbell, R., Swettenham, J., Hansen, P. and Ramus, F. (2006) 'Motion and form coherence detection in autistic spectrum disorder: relationship to motor control and 2:4 digit ratio.' *Journal of Autism and Developmental Disorders 36*, 2, 225–237.

Mindick, N. (2005a) 'Resolution theory,' unpublished manuscript, presented at Harvard Graduate School of Education Conference, January.

Pietz, J., Ebinger, F. and Rating, D. (2003) 'Prosopagnosia in a preschool child with Asperger syndrome.' *Developmental Medicine and Child Neurology 45*, 1, 55–57.

Stein J. (2003) 'Visual motion sensitivity and reading.' *Neuropsychologia 41*, 1785–1793.

Vandenbroucke, M. Scholte, H.S., Enegland, H., Lamme, V. and Kemner, C. (2008) 'Coherent versus component motion perception in autism spectrum disorder.' *Journal of Autism and Developmental Disorders 38*, 5, 941–949.

## CHAPTER 5

Alperin, G. (n.d.) *Prosopagnosia: An Introduction to and FAQ about a Most Peculiar Condition*. Available at www.home.earthlink.net/~blankface/prosopagnosia.shtml, accessed on 24 May 2010.

Burman, C. (n.d.) *Welcome to my Pages about Prosopagnosia*. Available at www.prosopagnosia.com/, accessed on 24 May 2010.

Choisser, B. (1997) *Face Blind!* Available at www.choisser.com/faceblind, accessed on 25 May 2010.

## CHAPTER 6

Alperin, G. (n.d.) *Prosopagnosia: An Introduction to and FAQ about a Most Peculiar Condition*. Available at www.home.earthlink.net/~blankface/prosopagnosia.shtml, accessed on 24 May 2010.

Burman, C. (n.d.) *Welcome to my Pages about Prosopagnosia*. Available at www.prosopagnosia.com/, accessed on 24 May 2010.

Busigny, T., Joubert, S., Felician, O., and Rossion, B. (2008). 'Processing upright and inverted faces in acquired prosopagnosic patients with no object recognition deficits' [Abstract]. *Journal of Vision 8*, 6, 156, 156a.

Choisser, B. (1997) *Face Blind!* Available at www.choisser.com/faceblind, accessed on 25 May 2010.

Farah, M., Wilson, K., Drain, M. and Tanaka, J. (1995) 'The inverted face inversion effect in prosopagnosia: evidence for mandatory, face-specific perceptual mechanisms.' *Vision Research 35*, 14, 2089–2093.

Gardner, H. (1993) *Multiple Intelligences: The Theory in Practice*. New York: Basic Books.

Karmiloff-Smith, A. (1998) 'Development itself is the key to understanding developmental disorders.' *Trends in Cognitive Sciences 2*, 10, 389–397.

Le Grand, R., Mondloch, C.J., Maurer, D. and Brent, H.P. (2004) 'Impairment in holistic face processing following early visual deprivation.' *Psychological Science 15*, 11, 762–768.

Minsky, M. (2006) *The Emotion Machine*. New York: Simon and Schuster.

Otsuka, Y., Nakato, E., Kanazawa, S., Masami, K. *et al.* (2007) 'Neural activation to upright and inverted faces in infants measured by near infrared spectroscopy.' *NeuroImage 34*, 1, 399–406.

Turati, C., Sangrigoli, S., Ruel, J., de Schonen, S. (2004) Evidence of the Face Inversion Effect in 4-Month-Old Infants. *Infancy, 6*, 2, 275–297

Schwarzer, G. Zauner, N. and Jovanovic, B. (2007) 'Evidence of a shift from featural to configural face processing in infancy'. *Developmental Science, 10*, 452–463.

## CHAPTER 7

Alperin, G. (2002) Untitled document. Available at www.home.earthlink.net/~blankface/uniform.html, accessed on 27 May 2010.

Barron, S. and Grandin, T. (2005) *The Unwritten Rules of Social Relationships: Decoding Social Mysteries Through the Unique Perspectives of Autism.* Arlington, TX: Future Horizons.

Duchaine, B., Parker, H. and Nakayama, K. (2003) 'Normal recognition of emotion in a prosopagnosic.' *Perception* 32, 827–838.

Ellemberg, D., Lewis, T., Defina, N., Maurer, D. *et al.* (2005) 'Greater losses in sensitivity to second-order local motion than to first-order local motion after early visual deprivation in humans.' *Vision Research 45*, 2877–2884.

Grandin, T. (2006) *Thinking In Pictures, Expanded Edition: My Life with Autism.* New York: Vintage Books.

Maslow, A.H. (1943) 'A theory of human motivation.' *Psychological Review 50*, 370–396. Available at www.psychclassics.yorku.ca/Maslow/motivation.htm, accessed on 27 May 2010.

Milne, E. White, S., Campbell, R., Swettenham, J., Hansen, P. and Ramus, F. (2006) 'Motion and form coherence detection in autistic spectrum disorders: relationship to motor control and 2:4 digit ratio.' *Journal of Autism and Developmental Disorders 36*, 2, 225–237.

## CHAPTER 8

Barron, S. and Grandin, T. (2005) *The Unwritten Rules of Social Relationships: Decoding Social Mysteries Through the Unique Perspectives of Autism.* Arlington, TX: Future Horizons.

## CHAPTER 9

Maslow, A.H (1943) 'A theory of human motivation.' *Psychological Review 50*, 370–396. Available at www.psychclassics.yorku.ca/Maslow/motivation.htm, accessed on 27 May 2010.

## CHAPTER 10

Alperin, G. (2002) Untitled document. Available at www.home.earthlink.net/~blankface/uniform.html, accessed on 27 May 2010.

Kennerknecht, I., Grüter, T., Welling, B., Wentzek, S. *et al.* (2006) 'First report of prevalence of non-syndromic hereditary prosopagnosia (HPA).' *American Journal of Medical Genetics Part A 140A*, 1617–1622.

Maslow, A.H (1943) 'A theory of human motivation.' *Psychological Review 50*, 370–396. Available at www.psychclassics.yorku.ca/Maslow/motivation.htm, accessed on 27 May 2010.


## CHAPTER 11

Alperin, G. (n.d.) *Prosopagnosia: An Introduction to and FAQ about a Most Peculiar Condition*. Available at http://home.earthlink.net/~blankface/prosopagnosia.shtml, accessed on 24 May 2010.

Burman, C. (n.d.) *Welcome to my Pages about Prosopagnosia*. Available at www.prosop-agnosia.com/, accessed on 24 May 2010.

Choisser, B. (1997) *Face Blind!* Available at www.choisser.com/faceblind/, accessed on 25 May 2010.


## CHAPTER 12

Adolphs, R. (2006) 'Perception and emotion: how we recognize facial expressions.' *Current Directions in Psychological Science 15*, 5, 222–226.

Barnes, M.L. and Sternberg, R.J. (1989) 'Social intelligence and decoding of nonverbal cues.' *Intelligence 13*, 263–287.

Baron-Cohen, S. (n.d.) Mind Reading: The Interactive Guide to Emotions. Available at www.jkp.com/mindreading, accessed on 27 May 2010.

Baron-Cohen, S. (1999) 'Social intelligence in the normal and autistic brain: an FMRI study.' *European Journal of Neuroscience II*, 1891–1898.

Bower, B. (2003) 'Vision seekers, giving eyesight to the blind raises questions about how people see.' *Science News Online 164*, 21. Available at www.sciencenews.org/articles/20031122/bob9.asp, accessed on 2 August 2005.

Camras, L.A. and Allison, K. (1985) 'Children's understanding of emotional facial expressions and verbal labels.' *Journal of Nonverbal Behavior 9*, 2, 84–94.

Cunningham, D.W. and Wallraven, C. (2009) 'Dynamic information for the recognition of conversational expressions.' *Journal of Vision 9*, 13, 1–17.

Dance, A. (2009) *Teaching Autistic Kids to Read Facial Expressions*. Available at www.articles.latimes.com/2009/apr/13/health/he-autism13, accessed on 27 May 2010.

Dehaene, S. (n.d.) *What are Numbers, Really? A Cerebral Basis for Number Sense*. Available at www.edge.org/3rd_culture/dehaene, accessed on 15 May 2004.

Duchaine, B., Parker, H. and Nakayama, K. (2003) 'Normal recognition of emotion in a prosopagnosic.' *Perception 32*, 827–838.

Ekman, P. (2003) *Emotions Revealed*. New York: Times Books.

Gardner, H. (1993) *Multiple Intelligences*. New York: Basic Books.

Hersen, M., Van Hasselt, V. and Segal, D. (1995) 'Social adaptation in older visually impaired adults: some comments.' *Social Psychology Quarterly 1*, 1, 49–60.

Lindner, J.L. and Rosen, L.A. (2006) 'Decoding of emotion through facial expression, prosody and verbal content in children and adolescents with Asperger syndrome.' *Journal of Autism and Developmental Disorders 36*, 6, 769–777.

Marshall, M.J. and Peck, D.F. (1986) 'Facial expression training in blind adolescents using EMG feedback: a multiple-baseline study.' *Behaviour Research and Therapy 24*, 4, 429–435.

Mindick, N. (2005b) 'Adaptation to new senses,' unpublished manuscript presented at Harvard Graduate School of Education Conference, January.

Minsky, M. (2006) *The Emotion Machine*. New York: Simon and Schuster.

Pierce, B. (2006) *The Blind Child: Part of the Family, Part of the World*. Available at www.nfb.org/Images/nfb/Publications/fr/fr21/fr06ws18.htm, accessed on 27 May 2010.

Stone Mountain Software (2008) *Gaining Face for Aspergers*. Available at www.true-needs.com/software/549, accessed on 27 May 2010.

The Massachusetts Institute of Technology Media Laboratory (n.d.) *Social Emotional Sensing Toolkit*. Available at www.affect.media.mit.edu/projectpages/esp, accessed on 27 May 2010.

Thirion-Marissiaux, A.F. and Nader-Grosbois, N. (2008) 'Theory of Mind "emotion", developmental characteristics and social understanding in children and adolescents with intellectual disabilities.' *Research in Developmental Disabilities 29*, 5, 414–430.

# CHAPTER 13

Anastas, J.S. and Rhodes, M.G. (2005) 'An own-age bias in face recognition for children and older adults.' *Psychonomic Bulletin and Review 12*, 6, 1043–1047. Available at www.lamar.colostate.edu/~mrhodes/AR05.pdf, accessed on 27 May 2010.

Duchaine, B. and Nakayama, K. (2004) 'Brief communications developmental prosopagnosia and the Benton Facial Recognition Test.' *Neurology 62*, 1219–1220.

Ekman, P. (2003) *Emotions Revealed*. New York: Times Books.

Kaufman, N.L. and Kaufman, A.S. (2004) *Kaufman Assessment Battery for Children*, second edition (KABC-II). Available at www.psychcorp.co.uk/Psychology/Child-CognitionNeuropschologyandLanguage/ChildGeneralAbilities/KaufmannAssessmentBatteryfor ChildrenSecondEdition(KABC-II).aspx, accessed on 27 May 2010.

# CHAPTER 14

Bower, B. (2003) 'Vision seekers, giving eyesight to the blind raises questions about how people see.' *Science News Online 164*, 21. Available at www.sciencenews.org/articles/20031122/bob9.asp, accessed on 2 August 2005.

Cannino, J., Cotton, R. and Torneo, E. (2009) *Picking Cotton: Our Memoir of Injustice and Redemption*. New York: St. Martin's Press

Cochlear implants (2004) Virginia Merrill Bloedel Hearing Research Center. Available at www.depts.washington.edu/hearing/cochlear_implant.php, accessed on 31 January 2005.

Devaul, R. (2003) *The Memory Glasses Project*. Available at www.media.mit.edu/wearables/mithril/memory-glasses.html, accessed on 9 February 2005.

Food and Drug Administration (FDA) (2009) *Cochlear Implants*. Available at www.fda.gov/cdrh/cochlear/whatare.html, accessed on 27 May 2010.

Gregory, R. and Wallace, J. (1963) *Recovery from Early Blindness: A Case Study*. Available at www.richardgregory.org/papers/recovery_blind/recovery-from-early-blindness.pdf, accessed on 8 February 2005.

Hier, D.B., Mondlock, J. and Caplan, L.R. (1983) 'Recovery of behavioral abnormalities after right hemisphere stroke.' *Neurology 33*, 3, 345–50.

Kennerknecht, I., Grueter, T., Welling, B., Wentzek, S. *et al.* (2006) 'First report of prevalence of non-syndromic hereditary prosopagnosia (HPA).' *American Journal of Medical Genetics Part A 140A*, 1617–1622.

Le Grand, R., Mondloch, C.J., Maurer, D. and Brent, H.P. (2004) 'Impairment in holistic face processing following early visual deprivation.' *Psychological Science 15*, 11, 762–768.

Listen Up (n.d.) *Cochlear Implants*. Available at www.listen-up.org/h_books/implants.htm, accessed on 27 May 2010.

McGraw, P. (n.d.) *Could you be an Eyewitness? Part 2*. Available at www.drphil.com/shows/show/1400, accessed on 27 May 2010.

Mindick, N. (2005b) 'Adaptation to new senses.' Unpublished manuscript presented at Harvard Graduate School of Education Conference, January.

Minsky, M. (2007) *The Emotion Machine*. New York: Simon and Schuster.

Morgan, C.A III, Hazlett, G., Baranoski, M., Doran, A., Southwick, S. and Loftus, E. (2007) 'Accuracy of eyewitness identification is significantly associated with performance on a standardized test of face recognition.' *International Journal of Law and Psychiatry 30*, 3, 213–223.

National Institute on Deafness and Other Communication Disorders (NIDCD) (2009) *Cochlear implants*. Available at www.nidcd.nih.gov/health/hearing/coch.asp, accessed on 27 May 2010.

Von Sender, M. (1960) *Space and Sight*. Glencoe: The Free Press.

# APPENDIX

Aslin, D. (1993) 'Infant Accommodation and Convergence.' In K. Simons (ed.) *Early Visual Development Normal and Abnormal*. New York: Oxford University Press.

Bell, G. and Gemmell, J. (2009) *Socrates on the Impact of Technology for Memories*. Available at www.totalrecallbook.com/blog/2009/12/21/socrates-on-the-impact-of-technology-for-memories.html, accessed on 27 May 2010.

Braddick, O., Atkinson, J., French, J. and Howland, H.C. (1979) 'Photorefractive study of infant accommodation.' *Vision Research 19*, 1319–1330.

Brookman, K.E. (ed.) (1983) 'Ocular Accommodation in Human Infants.' *American Journal of Optometry and Physiological Optics 60*, 2, 91–99.

Dehaene, S. (n.d.) *What are Numbers, Really? A Cerebral Basis for Number Sense.* Available at www.edge.org/3rd_culture/dehaene, accessed on 15 May 2004.

Ellemberg, D., Lewis, T., Defina, N., Maurer, D. *et al.* (2005) 'Greater losses in sensitivity to second-order local motion than to first-order local motion after early visual deprivation in humans.' *Vision Research 45*, 2877–2884.

Freitag, C.M., Konrad, C., Häberlen, M., Kleser, C. *et al.* (2008) 'Perception of biological motion in autism spectrum disorders.' *Neuropsychologia 46*, 5, 1480–1494.

Haynes, H., White, B.L. and Held, R. (1965) 'Visual accommodation in human infants.' *Science 148*, 3669, 528–530.

Mindick, N. (2005a) 'Resolution theory,' unpublished manuscript, Soon to be available, presented at Harvard Graduate School of Education conference, January.

Mindick, N. (2005b) 'Adaptation to new senses,' unpublished manuscript, Soon to be available, presented at Harvard Graduate School of Education conference, January.

Mindick, N. (2005c) 'The case for an alternative math symbol system,' unpublished manuscript, soon to be available, presented at Havard Graduate School of Education conference, January.

Mindick, N. (2005d) 'Dyslexia among Braille readers,' unpublished manuscript, soon to be available.

Stein J. (2003) 'Visual motion sensitivity and reading.' *Neuropsychologia 41*, 1785–1793.

Vandenbroucke, M., Scholte, H.S., Engeland, H., Lamme, V. and Kemner, C. (2008) 'Coherent versus component motion perception in autism spectrum disorder.' *Journal of Autism and Developmental Disorders 38*, 5, 941–949.

# SUBJECT INDEX

# AUTHOR INDEX

CPI Antony Rowe
Eastbourne, UK
June 20, 2023